fab

boarding cattery manual

Edited by Claire Bessant

Published by the
Feline Advisory Bureau
Taeselbury
High Street
TISBURY
Wiltshire SP3 6LD

Designed by
Tony Baldwin
TISBURY Wiltshire

Printed by
Blackmore Ltd
Shaftesbury Dorset

Front cover picture
Warren Photographic

ISBN 0 9533942 1 2

Sponsored by

feline advisory bureau
boarding cattery

manual contents

feline advisory bureau
boarding cattery

manual contents

FAB and boarding catteries

One of the objectives of FAB when it was set up in 1958 was to improve the standards of boarding catteries. At that time there were no guidelines at all for anyone wishing to board cats and there were many appalling boarding establishments. Through the work of a few dedicated people, FAB began to develop the ideas for the design, construction and management of catteries to ensure the safety and care of the cats. It was not until 1963 that the Animal Boarding Establishments Act was introduced. Although this stipulated that a licence was required to run a boarding cattery, it gave no information on standards and how they could be achieved. In 1995 the Chartered Institute of Environmental Health introduced its Model Licence Conditions and Guidance for Cat Boarding Establishments (into which FAB had some input) which goes into much greater detail about cattery construction. This is the document which is used to gauge whether catteries should be licensed by the local authority.

FAB has been publishing information and a manual of cattery design, construction and management since its early days. This new manual is the result of the collaboration between a large number of people with many different talents. It explains why certain aspects of design and management are important and how best cats should be cared for in the cattery environment. FAB has always prided itself on its standards and alongside this Boarding Cattery Manual is printed the FAB Standard for Construction and Management of Boarding Catteries 2002. This document explains what is required in order to be accepted onto the FAB Listing Scheme, under which catteries are inspected by FAB to ensure they conform to the highest standards of cattery care. The Manual explains how the items laid out in the Standard can be achieved. Working drawings are also available for those wishing to build an outdoor wooden cattery. For more information on the FAB Standard, FAB Listing Scheme and working drawings, contact FAB at:

FAB Boarding Cattery Information
Taeselbury
High Street
Tisbury
Wilts SP3 6LD

Tel: 0870 742 2278
Fax: 01747 871873
Email: catteries@fabcats.org
Website: www.fabcats.org

Also available on the website or as leaflets is 'Choosing a good boarding cattery' - a guide which explains what to look for when visiting a boarding cattery.

Introduction

The Feline Advisory Bureau has been working to improve the care of cats for over 40 years. It has been instrumental in many of the improvements which have been made in the standard of boarding catteries over the years. This new version of the long admired Boarding Cattery Construction and Management Manual adds further to the knowledge of cat care in the cattery situation. Although it is written to help cattery proprietors run a good business, it makes no apology to have as its main remit the health and welfare of the cats boarded in the cattery. As proprietors of our FAB Listed Catteries have found, owners appreciate their care and knowledge and return again and again, booking cats in well in advance to ensure a place – so excellent standards do pay off in business terms too. Owners want to be sure that they are leaving their cat, a member of the family, in safe and caring hands.

High standards are not necessarily about luxury – keeping design and construction as simple and practical as possible will allow for ease of care and cleaning. Giving cats warmth and space to exercise and providing a caring environment is much more important than trying to emulate the owner's home. While owners may think they like the idea of soft furnishing and a home from home environment, they may not understand the added risk of passing on infections that this can bring.

This manual set outs the principles of good design and management, aimed at minimising the risks to cats in a cattery of infectious disease, injury, loss or depression and to maximise the care given to them. It explains why these requirements are necessary and how they can be achieved. Different designs of cattery are possible and will keep changing in the future – the important thing is always to consider what the design is for and to aim to keep cats safe and make the care of them as straightforward as possible for the proprietors.

This manual has been written alongside our brand new, original FAB Standard for Construction and Management of Boarding Catteries 2002, which sets out the salient requirements for design and management. This Standard will become the basis for assessment, under which a cattery can be accepted for FAB Listing.

Acknowledgements

It has taken a great deal of team work and collaboration to bring the information in this manual together. People have contributed words, pictures, advice, diagrams and their time. FAB would like to thank everyone for their commitment and enthusiasm in working to raise the standards of boarding catteries through the high quality information which has been brought together.

Thank you to all the people involved in putting the contents of this manual together.
The main contributors were Sarah Caney, Sally Franklin, Hugh Guilford, Gill Waldron, Claire Bessant, Jean Gillespie and Jenny Parkhouse.

Thank you to Jane Burton of Warren Photographic for letting FAB use her beautiful picture of a tabby for the front cover and to Paddy Cutts for her pictures of grooming and bathing cats.

Thank you to the following who have contributed by building the beautiful catteries which are shown in the manual and providing some of the pictures: Eastham Woods Boarding Cattery, Wirral - The Cats Whiskers, Staffordshire - Country Club Cattery, Scotland - Treetops Cattery, Devon - Pampered Paws Cattery, Suffolk - Littledowns Cattery, Somerset - Hillhouse Boarding Cattery, Scotland - Harriets Hotel Boarding Cattery, Worcestershire - Blue Cross, Torbay - The Cats Whiskers, Worcestershire - Martlets Cattery, East Sussex - The Cats Whiskers, Northamptonshire – Bucklyvie Cottage Cattery, Scotland - Pinewood Cattery, Surrey - Halls Cross Cattery, East Sussex - Cosy Cats Boarding Cattery, Nottinghamshire - The Country Cattery, Kent - Ferndene Cattery, Northumberland - Colinton Country Cattery, Scotland - Adwick Cats Lodge, Yorkshire - Ivanlea Boarding Cattery, Scotland – Cuddington Boarding Cattery, Cheshire – Stonehenge Cats Hotel, Wiltshire - Specialcats of Ayr, Scotland

Thank you to the following who have contributed pictures for the veterinary section:
Sarah Caney, Aiden Foster, Ann Robinson, Geoff Lane, Langford Feline Centre, Bayer and the owners of Tiggy Mitchell.

And finally
This manual has been based on the pioneering work done for FAB by Joan Judd, Mary White, Sophie Hamilton-Moore and Caryl Cruickshank in raising the standards of design and management of catteries. Their vision and determination to improve the care of cats in catteries cannot be underestimated.

CHAPTER 1

Before you start

Look upon this section as a signpost giving you directions for a journey into the unknown. Your final 'destination' would be reached on becoming the proprietor of a boarding cattery. Before setting off on a difficult trip, it is always sensible to make plans. The first part of this chapter focuses on the main issues for planning BUT, before going any further, take the time to convince yourself that you should be travelling at all! The rest of this chapter is to help you address this question:
Are you sure that you should be starting up a cattery?

Running a boarding cattery can be both rewarding and fulfilling — if you have the commitment and stamina. Caring for other people's pets is a big responsibility and it takes dedication to cope with the long days and the hard physical work. A cattery represents a large call on your time; however, if it is the life for you then you will gain great satisfaction from establishing and running a high quality cattery.

Seek out as much information as possible. It is worth viewing a selection of catteries as there are different styles and designs. Try and include one of those catteries which have FAB Listing to give you an idea of good construction and management. It can be all too easy to take on or build a poor quality cattery if you have not done your research. Be sure there is sufficient business available in your location and catchment.

If you buy an existing cattery this should give you an established client list. You should also be free of planning permission applications. Buying a home and business together may be a large financial outlay. If considering this route the cattery should at least conform to the CIEH Model Licence Conditions. Local authorities are now enforcing these standards and may not licence a cattery if they feel it does not comply with these guidelines.

Certain buildings, for example wooden stable blocks, can be converted into cattery accommodation although this option can sometimes prove to be very expensive. Bear in mind you may need to apply for planning permission for 'change of use' and any conversion should follow the same principles of good design.

Many people decide to erect a cattery either on their current property or on the land of a newly purchased house. Before purchasing a new property it is advisable that you check with the local authorities to ensure that they will permit you to build a cattery of the size you desire on the site.

Regulations
All boarding establishments are required to be licensed by the local authority under the Animal Boarding Establishments Act of 1963. The licence, which is granted in the name of the owner, is issued annually and renewed on 1st January. All catteries must have a current licence.

Your local authority may attach conditions to the licence and use the Chartered Institute of Environmental Health (CIEH) Model Licence Conditions & Guidance for Cat Boarding Establishments (1995) as a guide (see Appendix A). Alternatively, they may adapt these guidelines to suit their own requirements.

During the year your local authority will usually make one or more visits to inspect your premises and this is normally carried out by an officer from the Environmental Health Department or a veterinary surgeon appointed by the local authority.

The licence fee, which is decided by each individual local authority, can vary enormously. However, the level of fees may be challenged if considered to be excessive. If you are planning to purchase an existing cattery, you should check the terms of the licence, as the licence is issued to the owner personally rather than the business. It is important to find out if there are any reasons why the licence might not be renewed and to obtain permission in writing from the local authority to transfer the licence to your name.

Planning permission
If you plan to build a new cattery you will need to apply to your local authority for outline and detailed planning permission, which can sometimes be a lengthy process. The local authority will provide the necessary paperwork and advise on how to proceed. Building Regulations may apply to specific types of catteries. You may care to engage the services of a professional architect to draw up plans for you, or do the work yourself. FAB's working drawings for certain styles of cattery can be used to support your planning application. If employing a specialist cattery builder to construct your cattery, they will usually offer a complete package and make a planning application on your behalf.

If your planning application is turned down by the local authority, it is possible to appeal. Your local authority should provide you with written reasons for the refusal.

A lifestyle rather than a job
Running a cattery is a way of life. Your clients will place complete trust in you and rely on you for absolute security

and excellent care for their cats. Living on site is strongly recommended to ensure the smooth running of the cattery and it should never be left unattended for more than short periods of time when cats are in residence.

The busiest times in the cattery calendar are the times when everyone else is off on holiday! Bank holidays, school holidays and Christmas will obviously be your peak periods and you will find that as your reputation is established, quiet times become increasingly scarce.

If you have young children or other dependants who need care, think carefully about the feasibility of starting a cattery as the necessary early starts and weekend work can also present problems. Taking a holiday and having a social life can also be difficult. It is possible to close down for short periods through the year if these are carefully planned. An alternative would be to employ someone totally reliable, well trained and familiar with your cattery to stand in for you.

Although running a boarding cattery is all about cats, a great deal of time is spent talking to and reassuring owners and maintaining a high quality business image. Ability to communicate clearly and calmly is vital. If you do not like people this is not the job for you!

Taking on a cattery requires a large financial outlay and although it is possible to make a reasonable living you may not necessarily make a fortune! Do work through a business plan and take advice on finance and all that is involved.

Qualifications and training
No formal qualifications are needed to run a cattery at the present time, although it is a great advantage for any cattery proprietor to have training in cattery management. The FAB can provide you with information on courses.

An active occupation
It is certainly necessary to be fit and active to run a cattery as daily tasks will include cleaning of every occupied unit, preparation and delivery of at least two meals, administration of any medicines, grooming, scrubbing and disinfection of units between boarders, updating of daily records and business paperwork, dealing with arrivals and departures, and general cattery cleaning. There is a great deal of bending, stretching and lifting involved. It is often an outdoor lifestyle – sometimes in bad weather conditions.

Other tasks to be fitted into the work programme will include maintenance of cattery buildings and gardens, along with bulk shopping and overall business management (ie, annual accounts).

If you are nearing retirement age or planning early retirement, do consider how long you intend to run the business. The need for assistance if you become unwell or less active should be considered.

Should you take the plunge?
It is of the utmost importance and benefit to the cats who need boarding in your area that the catteries available to them are well-run and successful. It is, of course, also important to the proprietors and to the owners of the cats, but the well-being of the cats comes top of the priority list! FAB does not want catteries to fail; proprietors to struggle; and standards to drop; because along the way it is inevitable that the boarding cats will lose out, even suffer, as a consequence. We therefore urge that the first stage of planning by anyone thinking of starting up their first boarding cattery is to go through a process of thinking through the

concept, the idea, and the scheme to satisfy themselves that they really are doing the right thing for them at the right time.

The thought process
As with all planning exercises, first write down your assumptions about the issue; in this case whether you really want to do this. This will oblige you to face up to the more difficult matters! Having done so, set about convincing yourself that this is for you. One approach to this is to address three fundamental questions that must (ought to!) be applied to any new business or new product line under consideration.

◆ Is it REAL?
◆ Can we WIN?
◆ Is it WORTHWHILE?

What do these three questions mean in the context of someone, with limited experience of starting and running his/her own small commercial venture, considering becoming a boarding cattery proprietor?

Is it REAL?
Is your concept of a service one that is realistic, meeting a real demand in your area?

The service: Is it realistic for you to create and run a cattery that offers boarding facilities to cats whose owners live nearby?

The demand: Is there a need locally from cat owners for boarding for their cats?

It is quite likely that the answers to both of these questions are affirmative, provided that the financial investment for setting up the cattery and coping with the negative cash flow during start up are both within your means. More on the financial challenges in Chapter 2, but if you can satisfy yourself that 'it' can indeed be REAL, then move on to the next question.

Can we WIN?
This is largely a competitive issue. There are normally two dimensions:

1 In the circumstances in your area, is it possible for *any* new cattery to succeed?
◆ Are there already too many catteries? Does supply already outstrip demand?
◆ Is your area so remote that the feline population is too thinly spread to keep another cattery at satisfactory occupancy year-round?

2 If so, can *your* cattery succeed in the face of whatever competition exists from existing catteries?
◆ Why would owners choose you?
◆ If they do board with you once, will they (want to) keep coming back?
◆ What differentiates your cattery? What are its USPs (Unique Selling Points)?

The answer to questions about winning and local competitiveness are less predictable than those about reality of service and demand. These are questions that you must do your best to answer for yourself. Remember, knowledge is everything! Rely as little as possible on guesswork, presumption and especially wishful thinking. Find out facts from as many different sources as you can. Ask! It is astonishing how readily most people will reveal what you want to know, even when the information ought to be confidential.

Is it WORTHWHILE?
The two key aspects to this are:
◆ Can the enterprise - in this case, your cattery - be profitable?
◆ Would running a successful cattery venture satisfy your own personal goals?

Profitability

Considerations of profitability can be somewhat different from the normal criteria for most businesses. This is because by no means everyone who runs a successful cattery does so primarily for profit.

Many catteries are well run very successfully as the primary source of income. Very, very few people get seriously rich by doing so! For significant numbers, however, this is more of a (fulltime) hobby that also generates a modest cash surplus. In some cases the cattery is the secondary source of income in a household where the other partner is gainfully employed as the main contributing breadwinner. Irrespective of your own goals for income, however, catteries cannot be run part-time, on the side!

Only you can know into which category you fall. But it does follow from these considerations that are characteristic of boarding cattery enterprises that the answer to the first part of the 'Worthwhile' question depends on what level of surplus is acceptable to your circumstances. From FAB's perspective, in which feline well-being is paramount, the answer is immaterial, provided your financial goals are achievable and being achieved.

Personal satisfaction

Running a cattery is very demanding, irrespective of whether you are seeking a huge profit or a modest surplus, or will be satisfied with just breaking even. There are life-style questions that you must face up to:

◆ Are you passionate about cats and their welfare, even when they are spiteful, unwell or smelly with mucky bums?
◆ Boarding the cats that you adore means dealing with their owners - some of them will not be so adorable! Can you cope with that?
◆ Have you got the support of your nearest and dearest?
◆ Will that support continue when the stark reality of the commitment and routine becomes apparent?
◆ Are you up for the early mornings, long hours, menial tasks and some disruption to weekends?
◆ Do you realise how difficult it will become to get away for a holiday?
◆ Are you willing to be seriously out of pocket during the first year or longer, dealing with the stress that often comes with inexperience of managing a negative cash flow?
◆ Are you truly reconciled to not becoming rich?

If your answers to some of the above are negative, think again about what you intend to do! But if your answers are 'Yes, yes, I really want to do this' then do go on to Chapter 2. Your next step will be more detailed planning.

Planning to go ahead

So it's 'Yes, yes I want to do this' - excellent! Now you have to get on with your plans. The word 'your' is used advisedly, because FAB is not going to do it for you. In this chapter, however, there are some pointers to help you. They are based on experience with successful, small commercial enterprises, customised to be relevant to starting up a boarding cattery for the first time.

The good news is that, if you went through the exercise of Chapter 1 thoroughly, you will already have done much of the strategic work. If you didn't do it before, do it now. Do not pass on commercial planning. If you plan well and sort out the key factors for success right at the start, it is much less likely that things will go wrong later.

Assumptions

First, expand on an exercise that you began when reviewing whether to go ahead on your journey. Write down your assumptions about everything that might have an impact on your success or failure.

◆ Categorise them into those issues over which you have influence, eg, availability of funds; premises; new-build or purchase of existing cattery; staff and other help or work alone; your relevant skills and competence, or lack thereof; design/type of cattery.

◆ Consider those over which you have no influence, eg, how many cats live near you; how many get boarded; how good or poor are the other local catteries; seasonality of demand.

◆ When you do this, you will probably come up with some issues where you are unsure whether you would be able to influence them or not. Examples include established perception of boarding fees; willingness of owners to deliver their cats to you and/or collect them afterwards; location; planning permission.

The reason for this categorisation is that you can do something about those over which you have influence. You have to live with and operate alongside the factors that are outwith your control, whether you like them or not.

Codifying assumptions will help you do some things early on that are very important: Challenge your preconceptions!

◆ Recognise what you don't really know.

◆ Ask yourself the unpleasant questions.
◆ Recognise and face up to the reasons for possible failure.
◆ Get into focus what the downsides are.
◆ See what you can do about them!

It is common for beginners (and, sadly, those with experience) to concentrate on the factors that are in their favour, while shying away from those that are against them. This is understandable. We all tend to focus on what we are comfortable with, what comes easier and what we like. In business start-up, that can be a formula for failure. You must come to terms with the hard bits. Ignore the positives while doing this, unless you get too depressed from trying to deal with the discouraging issues. It can be good then for your morale to reflect on the positives, but they do tend to take care of themselves, with some effort from you of course, once you have sorted the negatives.

Business start-up factors

There are plenty of guides with help on business start-up. 'Planning for the Future' (*Kennel and Cattery Management* Feb 1999) is just one such useful source of general guidance. It puts together a checklist of issues to be considered for any commercial enterprise. It gives sound guidance on:
◆ The importance of cash flow;
◆ The value of researching the marketplace;
◆What will be needed to get ongoing financial support, if required?

Even this, however, does not succeed in making it at all clear which of the factors are key, most important for a cattery project. Much of that, as it impinges on you, was covered in the previous chapter.

Commercial planning matters

Pick up the themes set out in Chapter 1, which can be very useful for continuing your planning. As set out under the three fundamental questions was, of course, an oversimplification for the purpose of helping you challenge your ideas and reach a decision. For the next step, the more detailed aspects of the three headings that are particularly relevant to starting a boarding cattery and worth your researching in more depth are:

1 Reality of market demand
Can (enough of) the cat owners buy your services? Can they afford you?

Are they near enough?
Will (enough of) the cat owners buy your services (repeatedly)?
Do they perceive good value from your cattery?
Are they dissatisfied with their present cattery?

2 Is your pricing right?
This is not the same as being low priced! Learn to distinguish between what is affordable and what is cheap. Business starters often assume that they have to pitch their charges low. Sometimes, for competitive reasons they are right, but not always. Decide which sector of your local market you are focussed on. Well-off people own cats too. Some will be prepared to pay higher boarding fees if the perceived value for money is high. It is much easier to reduce your established prices than to put them up from a low base!

3 Is the risk worthwhile?
Could you cope with failure, losing your investment?
Don't put your property up as security of any loan.

Can you afford the up-front investment?
Before you can start making money, you will have to lay out lots of dosh. Even if your cattery is going to become profitable, it will take time to get established. In the meantime, you will be paying out more than you take in. One of the most common, and certainly most disastrous, errors that starters of new businesses make is in their assumptions about how soon they will start taking in money. It almost always takes longer than you expect!

Don't be averse to using other institution's money to finance your start up. But do be careful when you compare the cost of borrowing with the cost of using your own capital. Again, underestimating the time till your cash flow becomes positive can be crucial.

How much will it cost - budgets?
It depends on what 'it' is, of course, but part of it will be the cattery itself. FAB's consultations with suppliers give indicators. For a 12-unit cattery of 'approved' design and timber construction, with 9 standard units and 3 for families, a budget of around £22,000 is realistic. This would cover concrete base, units delivered and erected, flooring, utilities and connections, but not reception, kitchen facilities or an isolation unit. If you are self-sufficient enough to take the DIY option, this budget can be reduced. You could decide that your time need not be included in the costings.

Do make sure that your budget covers all outlays. These may include:
Staff (if any) - allow about 1.17 times wages for employment cost per capita.
Cost of borrowings - interest on overdraft (if any)
Equipment for the cattery
Landscaping and/or garden maintenance
Promotional and other marketing expenditure, including website
Stocks - food, litter, disinfectants, bedding etcetera
Stationery, office supplies and printing
Computer
Insurances
Business rates
Telephone and utilities [electricity, water]
Cattery maintenance and repairs
Vehicle (if any)
Professional fees (eg, accountant, bookkeeper)
Fees for licencing, planning permission

Funding or writing off bad debts
Membership and Listing with FAB

Marketing
This is a much misunderstood matter, in which there is great confusion with research, sales, price, promotion and publicity.

Marketing is the management skill of anticipating and meeting customer need profitably.

Research is the means by which you find out about and understand your marketplace. Remember to review your findings from before start-up at intervals in the future. Circumstances change. Most of the rest are tools of the trade, which you apply to achieve your marketing strategy.

You will have done your strategic marketing when challenging yourself about taking the plunge. To get to grips with the tactical side, decide on which of the many tools are appropriate to your venture. This is your marketing 'mix'. Let's consider some of the elements:

◆ **Research?** Yes, but you don't need costly help - do it yourself. Visit other catteries. Find out about fees; demand; seasonality; occupancy; services offered; are they FAB Listed? ASK.
◆ **Hire a sales force?** Surely not! Use your clients, they are much less expensive!
◆ **Customer service?** Essential for dealing with owners
◆ **Position?** More important in the retail world. You must be on or close to your cattery. There is unlikely to be much choice on where the cattery is to be sited. But access and parking must be considered.
◆ **Pricing?** Critical - see above.
◆ **Product?** Isn't that obvious? It's a cattery. Well, yes, but see below.
◆ **Promotion?** Yes, but by what means? See below.

There seem to be two matters that need to be looked at in more detail:
◆ What is your 'product'? ie, what services shall you offer?
◆ How best to promote your cattery, within budgetary constraints.

Service offer
Cattery alone? Opening hours? Collection service? Deliver the cats back to their owners? Veterinary link-up? If your interest is just in running a boarding cattery, these are the kind of product questions for you.

Kennels? Boarding for other small animals? Cat owners have hamsters too!

What about other income generators? Look at the synergy. You will have face-to-face access to the owners who spend money on their cats. Why not with you? Ancillary services such as grooming, hydrotherapy?

Arranging funeral services? Retail - selling on cat food, collars, ID tags, cat carriers etcetera? Cat dancing classes?

If diversification intrigues you, read 'Kennel Income' *Kennel and Cattery Management* July/August 2001. FAB does not object to a proprietor having income from sources other than boarding cats, provided that the care and well-being of the cats remains paramount. If you do decide to board other animals, it must be done in a way that does not distress or detract from the cats.

Promotion
Here are some thoughts that might help you use your time, effort and expenditure wisely and efficiently.

- Satisfied customers are your best advocates. They are your sales force! That's great because they are free of charge! Ask them to recommend you to their cat-owning friends. Beg them to keep bring their own cats back.
- A catchy name for your cattery can help.
- Use local media to publicise the opening of your cattery. Hold an open day event. Show off the premises. If you want to splash out, look into a slot on local or animal-based radio.
- Do a press release - it's a lot cheaper than advertising.
- Yours is a local business. Use local media to publicise the opening of your cattery.
- Make up business cards and compliments slips. Get them displayed in as many veterinary waiting rooms and village shop windows as will permit you. Get your milkman, paper shop delivery to drop them off, maybe in exchange for boarding their cats at no charge. In the local economy, barter trade has much to recommend it.
- Third party endorsement is good business. Owners have to trust you with their loved ones. To know that FAB endorses your establishment is a great basis for trust, especially if your competitors do not have the same endorsement. Point that out to the owners. Feature your listing on your literature, including invoices or receipts.
- Keep and display testimonials from satisfied customers.

Set up an efficient business administration

- Keep a day diary for telephone bookings.
- Use forms that enable you to take full details of your client owners and cats and how to contact them.
- Use either a good manual or computerised booking in and billing system. Avoid getting into bespoke software. It may sound cheaper, but it will let you down, becoming more trouble than it was worth.
- Make it easy for prospective clients to contact you and find you. Do a map on the back of your compliments slip. Put up a clear sign outside.

If you do get a complaint, deal with it directly with the owner. Find out what went wrong. See what you can do to prevent recurrence.

Many of these matters are covered in greater detail in the administration and management chapters later in this Manual. Part of your research should be to read the Manual to improve your knowledge of design and management that will, of course, need to be covered in your planning and costings.

CHAPTER 3

Principles of good cattery design

The designs and management ideas laid out in this manual are based on veterinary knowledge of disease control, ease of use and appreciation of what cats need in their environment. There are some basic principles which need to be incorporated into the way a cattery is designed. These are listed below and the following chapters lay out how these principles can be put into practice.

There are three main types of cattery. The same principles apply to each, but how they are achieved may vary slightly.

1 Outdoor catteries
Catteries with indoor sleeping accommodation and individual covered outdoor exercise runs - accessed individually from a covered, outdoor safety corridor.

2 Semi-outdoor catteries
Catteries with indoor sleeping accommodation and individual covered outdoor exercise runs - accessed individually from a common indoor corridor.

3 Indoor catteries
Catteries with indoor sleeping accommodation and indoor exercise runs - accessed individually from a common indoor corridor.

Principles of good cattery design
◆ Cat accommodation must comprise separate enclosed sleeping accommodation and an exercise run.
◆ Cat accommodation must be of appropriate size and be warm, dry and secure.
◆ There must be no possibility of cats within the cattery (excluding those from the same household in the same unit) coming into direct contact with each other.
◆ Only cats from the same household may be boarded together.
◆ Communal exercise areas are not acceptable.
◆ There must be no possibility of cats within the cattery coming into contact with any animal outside the cattery.
◆ The design is such that ventilation and air flow minimise the danger of spreading air-borne diseases.
◆ Cats must be safe from escape and injury
◆ Construction allows for ease of cleaning and disinfection of surfaces thus minimising the risk of passing on disease.
◆ Cats are kept warm or cool as required.
◆ Reception and food areas are sited and managed to minimise any cross infection.
◆ There is an isolation facility for use with ill or suspected ill cats.
◆ Elements of design of the unit, such as aspect, space and shelving are such that they minimise stress for the cats.

Why these principles are necessary and how they are achieved are outlined in the section below .

Minimising the risk factors for cats
What are the risks to a cat in a cattery?
◆ Infectious disease
◆ Escape
◆ Physical harm
◆ Boredom and depression

Risk of infectious diseases
Anyone who has had a large number of cats in one place will be aware of the potential for serious disease and will know problems escalate the more cats there are kept together. An animal's immune system can also be affected by any stress it is feeling, so that it may not be functioning at its best while the cat is at the cattery. Thus, unless your cattery has excellent hygiene protocols and the accommodation is designed so that cats cannot make contact with each other and pass on disease directly, the cats in your care could go home in a less healthy state than when they arrived. This would be upsetting for both owners and cats.

Cats can suffer from a variety of infectious diseases which can be passed from one cat to another. Some, like feline leukaemia (FeLV) and feline immunodeficiency virus (FIV), need direct contact between the cats. Others, such as enteritis can be passed on via handling, or can be airborne, like the cat flu viruses. Hence, the construction of a good cattery must take these into account and try to minimise potential problems by ensuring that:

◆ There are gaps between the units (minimum width 0.6 m) or, if units are joined together, full height sneeze barriers are present to prevent cats from different households having direct contact with each other or sneezing on one another.
◆ There is sufficient ventilation to prevent accumulation and circulation of shared air which may contain viruses and other infectious agents.
◆ Surfaces are smooth, easy to reach and clean.

Most catteries will approach the problem of providing adequate ventilation by building to allow a natural flow of air through the cattery. This is the great advantage of outdoor catteries which you will find referred to frequently in this manual. The provision of outdoor runs allows fresh air to flow through and between units and removes/dilutes any pockets of airborne viruses or bacteria. If proprietors wish to build a semi-outdoor or an indoor cattery the risks associated with a shared air supply must be considered. It is suggested that:

For a semi-outdoor cattery
◆ There is a solid door between the cat unit and the common indoor corridor
◆ There is ventilation through that corridor – this may be as simple as a window which opens at each end (covered with mesh to prevent accidental escape should a cat get into the corridor)
◆ Each cat's sleeping accommodation should be an independent unit – there should not be an obvious flow of air between units
◆ There must be a safety area at the end of the outdoor runs of at least 0.6m wide to ensure that outdoor cats and other animals cannot come into direct contact with the boarded cats

For an indoor cattery
◆ There is a solid door between the cat unit and the common indoor corridor
◆ There is ventilation through that corridor – this may be as simple as a window which opens at each end (covered with mesh to prevent accidental escape should a cat get into the corridor)
◆ Each unit must have solid doors, walls and ceiling

It is obvious from the above that the facility for air flow in a totally indoor cattery is limited. If poorly constructed, it can increase the risk of spreading airborne diseases. For this reason FAB has always preferred outdoor or semi-outdoor catteries. There may well be cause to recommend that indoor catteries should have some means of providing air exchanges – probably between three and six each hour – which would mean the use of a mechanical air exchange system.

Risk of escape
Every year there are reports in the press about owners going on holiday and returning to find that the cattery has 'lost' their cat. A properly constructed and maintained cattery with good management protocols should find it virtually impossible to lose a cat. On the construction side the possibility of escape can be minimised by ensuring that:

◆ Any outside run is completely enclosed with rigid wire mesh.
◆ Access to the cat unit is via a secure safety corridor or a secure area built in unison with the units. The doors should be securable both internally and externally.
◆ The safety corridor is completely enclosed with rigid wire mesh (including roof) and its door to the outside must be extra secure.
◆ The external door or gate to the safety corridor should be locked from the outside using a good quality padlock when there is nobody in the cattery, and be secured internally when it is in use.
◆ The cattery is maintained to the highest standards and any small holes in the wire mesh or broken door latches are fixed immediately.

Risk of physical harm
Be mindful of the possibilities for a cat to come to harm. This is distressing and a very poor reflection on your cattery. This problem can be avoided by:

◆ Making sure all cat flaps, shelves, trays and bed surfaces are smooth. Take care when positioning any items of furniture to eliminate the likelihood of a cat colliding with it and getting hurt when jumping or running.
◆ Removing collars from cats on arrival (especially those collars with loose attachments) to eliminate the possibility of the collar becoming caught in the wire mesh and harm the cat.

Risk of boredom and depression
In a boarding situation, cats can easily become bored or depressed. You may wonder how design and construction can have a part to play in this. In worrying about all of the construction details to prevent escape and a good hygiene regime, it can be easy to forget that the cats in the cattery could get bored or feel isolated in their pens. Cats are intelligent, active and social creatures who also have a great need for order. They need to have some visual stimulation as they lie on their shelves or watch out of the viewing window as well as being able to play etc. In a well designed cattery this can be achieved by providing:

◆ An initial design which ensures that the runs have an outlook onto an interesting area. Many catteries have a central area where they feed the birds or squirrels and grow plants which encourage butterflies and other insects to visit. These provide endless fascination for the cats.
◆ A design which allows the cats to see the people working in the cattery and provides interest in this way. Using see-through polycarbonate/perspex or similar material for sneeze barriers, rather than a solid wall or opaque material, allows cats to see each other too.
◆ A viewing window from the sleeping accommodation so that if it is too cold to sit out in an outside run in the winter, they can still see outside.
◆ Shelves in the runs for the cats to sun themselves on.
◆ Plenty of toys and different levels for the cats to play on.
◆ Facilities for scratching and sharpening of claws (eg, scratch posts) and different levels to climb on to enable cats to exhibit their natural behaviours.

CHAPTER 4

Principles into practice
Choice of site & type of cattery

Choice of site

Many people decide to build a cattery themselves either on their current property or on the land of a newly purchased house. Rural areas within reasonable driving distance of town or city are the most popular. It is sometimes possible to build in a residential area, however this depends entirely on the local authority. Aim for a catchment area of about 20 miles. It may seem quite a distance but people are often happy to travel to a good cattery.

Approximately quarter to a half an acre can be sufficient space to build a cattery of average size (roughly 20 units). If there is an excess of land the maintenance may prove costly in time, money and effort. It is important that the area around the cattery is neat and well cared for – many catteries have beautiful gardens or areas to attract birds.

An average sized cattery in a garden setting

On finding your ideal property, the first thing to do is to check with the Planning Department of the Local Authority whether the site is subject to restrictions such as green belt, conservation or preservation orders. Do some research on the number of catteries there are in the area (The Environmental Health Department of the Local Authority should be able to provide you with a list of the licensed catteries) – this will give you a good idea of your competition. It is not always a bad thing for there to be other catteries in the area. If there is quite a large population it is often possible to establish a relationship with other cattery owners, which can prove mutually beneficial. For example, if another cattery within travelling distance meets your standards you could recommend them as a back-up for yourself (and vice versa) in very busy periods.

Contacting any close neighbours and perhaps the local parish council to see how they feel about your project will help to avoid objections when your application goes in for planning permission. Common objections are noise, smell and an increase in traffic. Make sure that the site has good access from main roads with turning space for a few cars. This will eliminate problems with the Highways Department of the Local Authority.

Cattery size, design and materials

If you are building your cattery from scratch you will need to consider carefully the number of units you start with. Take into consideration your existing commitments, your time, and the cost of setting up. Check with the local Environmental Health Office for how many units you can apply to have licensed. It is often better to start with a manageable number of units and expand as you become more confident and experienced. Larger catteries will need staff as well as the proprietor – the costs will have to be weighed up in your business plan. Housing one to two cats (from the same household) in each unit and including a couple of family units will give you flexibility.

Choosing the right design and materials is very important - for you and for the cats. Be careful to check with the local authority - some have very strict rules on which materials you may use. Minimum requirements for licensing can be found in the Chartered Institute of Environmental Health (CIEH) Model Licence Conditions & Guidance for Cat Boarding Establishments or you can build to the FAB

Standard for Construction and Management of Boarding Catteries which incorporates the CIEH guidelines but has higher requirements in some areas. These are explained in this manual.

Siting and layout of the cattery

The way a cattery faces can have a major effect on how it withstands weather conditions, the temperature inside the cattery and therefore the environment to which both staff and cats are subjected. Try to make the best use of sunlight and use the building as a wind barrier.

A cattery facing south/south west will catch most of the available sunshine. Units with outside runs will be as dry and as bright as weather conditions allow and the cats won't miss out on their sun-bathing potential! Facing a cattery to the north will result in the back of the units receiving full heat in hot weather and the possibility of front-facing runs retaining the damp.

The most popular and successful layouts are the 'L' shape or the three sides of a square facing as southerly as is possible. This provides some shelter for the cattery, allows good circulation of air and the proprietor is able to make a feature of the middle area for the cats. The design also cuts down on walking.

If a back-to-back construction is used, an east/west orientation will allow maximum sunlight.

Building a cattery with a central corridor with runs facing inwards is not recommended – it will require roofing over the entire structure which will cut down on sun and make drying times longer. There is also a limited outlook for the cats.

Left: Cattery built in 'L' shape
Below left: Cattery built as a single row
Below: Cattery built in a 'U' shape (3 sides of a square)

Types of cattery

There are many different types and styles of cattery but most fall into three basic groups:

1 Outdoor catteries

Catteries with indoor sleeping accommodation and individual covered outdoor exercise runs - accessed individually from a covered, outdoor safety corridor.

Points to consider:
◆ This design has been by far the most popular with FAB cattery proprietor members
◆ The design is very attractive and allows for units to be constructed in pairs with a gap either side and full height barrier between, or joined together with full height sneeze barrier on both sides
◆ It allows for good access
◆ The outlook for the cats is interesting
◆ There is excellent airflow and ventilation which cuts down greatly the possibility of passing on diseases
◆ It can get cold for cattery workers (the cats have heating inside the sleeping accommodation!)

2 Semi-outdoor catteries

Catteries with indoor sleeping accommodation and individual covered outdoor exercise runs - accessed individually from a common indoor corridor.

Provided this design incorporates sufficient airflow through its indoor corridor to allow for changes in air to cut down the risk of spreading airborne disease, it is another completely successful design.

Points to consider:
◆ There should be some means of providing ventilation within the indoor corridor – this can be as simple as open mesh over a window at each end of the corridor or a mesh door.

Above: Typical 'outdoor' cattery showing gaps between units rather than sneeze barriers

Left and below: 'Semi-outdoor' cattery showing outdoor runs and safety corridor, and internal corridor

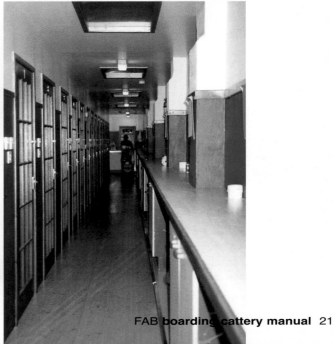

◆ There should be solid doors to the cat units opening into the corrridor with a shatterproof viewing panel.

◆ It provides a warmer working environment for cattery personnel.

◆ Runs should face outwards rather than inwards (these will have a full height sneeze barrier between).

◆ There needs to be a safety area at the end of the runs outside whether or not they have doors at that end too. This is to ensure that animals from outside cannot come into physical contact with the cats in the runs – this should be at least 0.6m wide. It is recommended that there is also access from the run end in case of fire.

◆ The internal corridor needs to be wide enough to allow movement along the corridor for people carrying equipment (such as cats in baskets), for people to pass each other and perhaps for disabled access. A good width would be 1.2 to 1.5 m wide.

3 Indoor catteries

Catteries with indoor sleeping accommodation and indoor exercise runs – accessed individually from a common indoor corridor.

In an indoor cattery cats are all housed under one roof but in separate compartments. The runs do not open into the outside air. The interior doors from the cat houses open on to an enclosed corridor or central passage.

Points to consider:

◆ This design has the advantage of extra warmth for workers and cats

◆ There is a potential large disadvantage of poor ventilation and shared air supply which can encourage spread of disease. It may require a mechanical means of providing permanent and variable ventilation which allows for adequate air exchange (3 to 6 changes per hour). Air exchange equipment must be investigated very thoroughly and professionally installed.

◆ There is little or no outlook for the cats unless there is a good viewing window to the outside.

Penthouse or full height sleeping accommodation?

Within this manual and the FAB Standard the accommodation for the cats is referred to as a 'unit' comprising sleeping accommodation and an exercise run. Within all of the categories the sleeping accommodation may comprise a full-height construction (walk-in) or a penthouse. Penthouses provide an enclosed boxed sleeping area raised off the ground. They are accessed by the cats using a ramp or solid ladder.

Both types have advantages and disadvantages - in the end it really does come down to individual choice. Visit catteries with each design and make careful note of what you see as the 'pro's and con's in the context of your own needs. Here are some points to consider:

◆ Usually in full-height units all areas can be easily reached and cleaned. When cleaning some penthouses it will be necessary to stand on a stool to reach all the way around inside and cleaning under the box may be difficult.

◆ Penthouses allow the separation of sleeping and toilet areas because the litter tray can be kept under the penthouse itself. This does mean that the cat has to leave the warm sleeping area and venture outside to use the tray (in full-height units the litter tray can be kept inside). Provision of a covered litter tray will allow the cat some privacy. Some penthouses are big enough to site the litter tray inside too.

◆ The height of the sleeping area in a penthouse may make special arrangements necessary when dealing with elderly, blind or infirm cats. Some catteries have one or two full height units for such cats – others ensure that the climb up into the penthouse is gentle and safe.

◆ A full height unit is safer with aggressive or frightened cats in that workers do not meet them at face height, as they can in a penthouse.

◆ If the penthouse is small it may not be high enough to accommodate the infra-red dull emitter type of heating which is a popular way of providing a warm environment for the cats.

Above: Full height sleeping accommodation **Above right:** Penthouse accommodation

Other components of cattery design include the kitchen, reception and isolation facilities, all of which are covered later in this manual.

Construction materials

Take time over choosing which materials you wish to build your cattery in. Contact as many suppliers as you can. You will find all of them helpful and their specialist knowledge will prove invaluable. When thinking over your choice, make a very detailed list of questions that you may have and use suppliers' answers in making your final judgment.

Also visit catteries and see how you like the construction 'in the flesh' and ask questions about ease of cleaning and maintenance. Many look fantastic – this will be the result of a lot of hard and constant work. You may decide to build yourself or get a local builder to build to a specific design (such as the FAB working drawings for a wooden cattery); you may be able to buy units from a manufacturer and construct them yourself, or you may wish to get a company to come in and do the whole lot for you. It comes down to time, money and talent at DIY!

Catteries are usually built using wood and/or brick/block or can be purchased as UPVC units. Each material has

Top left: Brick and wood **Top right:** Wooden construction **Above Left:** UPVC construction **Above right:** Cattery using galvanised mesh panels for run construction

advantages and disadvantages, and while the decision on which to use must rest with the cattery owner, it is worth noting the following points:

Points to consider:
1 Wood
◆ Most popular material - tried and tested.
◆ Must be pre-treated with a wood preservative
◆ Probably the cheapest material
◆ Can DIY or buy complete from a manufacturer or buy units and construct yourself
◆ Particularly attractive in rural setting
◆ Easy to add to
◆ Responds well to seasonal weather - cool in summer but warm in winter. Can be insulated sufficiently
◆ Needs very regular treatment with good quality safe wood preservers and careful continuing maintenance.
◆ Needs to be constructed from high quality timber for longevity
◆ Will accumulate algae and mould if not scrubbed often

Left: Example of full height outdoor wooden cattery cat accommodation showing viewing window and catflap into run. **Centre:** Example of a family size penthouse cat accommodation and run showing viewing window, sneeze barriers between pens, ramp into run and wire safety roof under the clear roofing. **Right:** Example of a full height uPVC cattery with viewing window, shelf, smooth flooring and safety corridor.

Genuine Pedigree Pens Installation

2 Half-brick/half-wood
◆ Can exceed life expectancy of all-wooden construction
◆ Much less maintenance
◆ May be difficult to insulate
◆ Can give superior draught/weather-proofing
◆ Can be constructed to blend in with houses
◆ May give opportunity for incorporated and sheltered storage areas
◆ Brickwork within the cat unit will require regular and full resealing to avoid infection risk
◆ Building regulations may apply
◆ DIY or combine with buying units from a manufacturer

3 uPVC
◆ Quickly installed
◆ Have erected for you or can buy flat-packs and DIY
◆ Smart appearance (particularly in urban setting)
◆ Resistant to algae and mould - requires less maintenance
◆ Available now in several colours – originally just white
◆ Easier surfaces to daily clean and disinfect

With the wooden or brick/block construction runs can be constructed with a wooden skeleton with mesh attached or from galvanised wire mesh panels.

Other activities on the site
How you site your cattery may also depend on what other activities may be going on at the site. The cattery must be positioned to minimise any of these which might cause the cats to be stressed or at risk because of noise/dust/smell or other activities. A good example of this is where the site also accommodates a kennelling facility for dogs. The noise and proximity of the dogs could be very upsetting for the cats. At FAB we prefer it if kennels are not on the same site, however, we have seen one or two where they are sufficiently far apart or there are buildings between which make the canine intrusion very minor.

Likewise if there is a rescue or breeding facility on the site this must be kept entirely separate from the boarded cats. It can be very difficult to ensure that people and equipment never cross from one area of work to the other. However, dual establishments are run, some very successfully. The important point to remember is that the risk of infection and the potential for upset and distress to all boarders is increased.

It is worth knowing that research has shown that clients do not favour dual establishments, regardless of the possible convenience. They prefer, in most cases, the security of knowing their animal is in a specialist establishment. Where other small pets are boarded these should be kept separate and their different requirements taken into account.

CHAPTER 5

Principles into practice
Basic requirements and ancillary buildings

The design of the building will split into several areas — the basic groundwork, the cat accommodation itself and the ancillary buildings. The cat accommodation will be considered separately in the next chapter.

Water supply

Water must be available either through mains or by the installation of standpipes. Hosing will be frequent. All measures to eliminate damage by fire must be accounted for.

Drainage - ground base

A properly constructed base is essential for all cat units and safety areas to ensure good drainage. While this may not seem to be a terribly exciting aspect of the construction, how it is done can have a huge effect on the volume of work and how pleasant or unpleasant the cattery work can be. If drainage is not correct, runs will be difficult to dry out after cleaning or hosing and puddles can form, all adding to the workload. All building must be in compliance with best building practice, ie, local authority guidelines, and be executed by a professional or very knowledgeable workman. Cattery units must be built on a concrete base with a damp proof membrane with carefully placed expansion joints occurring between runs. The concrete base, which must be a minimum of 100 mm thick, must be finished to a smooth, impervious surface which can easily be cleaned and

disinfected. Make sure it is constructed and maintained as to allow continued drainage and resist puddling of water. Base should have a fall of 75 mm to the front or rear to allow for ease of hosing away dirt and debris. Expansion joints should be placed at 3 m intervals and these should be placed so that they occur between the units. The size of the cat units (page 29) must be taken into account before laying the concrete pad so that the joints fall in the right places. Discuss your requirements fully with your builder as the need for a smooth surface for the concrete is vital.

Hosing should run into a properly installed drain, preferably part of the mains system. A French or soak-away drain is acceptable in cases where the amount of water is small - perhaps from a very small cattery or isolation unit - but it is advisable to have a full drainage system for the bulk of the cattery. The underside of a wooden construction should stand on rot-proof blocks to facilitate the escape of water. This is usually done using 20 mm high blocks of plastic which keep the structure off the ground and prevent moisture travelling up from the concrete into the wood.

Kitchen

A separate kitchen unit for cattery use only must be installed. The kitchen can be of the same basic construction as the bulk of the cattery and will indeed compliment the overall look of the complex if it is matched to cattery units in wood and colouring. If there is an existing utility room or outbuilding this can be utilised.

The kitchen must have sufficient room for the preparation of meals to be attended to in clean and organised surroundings. It is a good idea to have your kitchen door accessible from within the cattery safety passage as this assists in security and cuts down on walking. The room must have a hot and cold water supply and adequate drainage to mains drainage or an approved, localised sewage disposal system. Drainage should be through mains if a dishwasher is to be installed.

A cat kitchen must be equipped with a refrigerator for storage of medicines, specialist cat foods and leftovers. If you cook fresh foods, then obviously a

Partly constructed 'square' cattery showing level smooth concrete base

Above: Cattery kitchens

plenty of storage space - you will always have more equipment to house than you estimate. Bear in mind how much space would be taken up by the storage of carriers left with you by owners while their cat is with you. Good quality garden sheds are sufficient storage rooms. They can be made very attractive, blend in very well - particularly with all wooden catteries - and if well erected can give many years of good service with the minimum of maintenance.

Store sheds should be sited outside of the cattery safety passage. This will ensure that they do not become an added security risk area and they will be easily accessible many times during the day without cattery disturbance.

Reception

A smart and efficient reception area is one of the most useful tools in promoting custom. It represents your attitude and commitment to both new and potential customers and existing clients. A good quality garden shed, as with store units, will make a good reception area. Make sure that there is plenty of light and line or decorate the interior attractively. It is best not sited in the house so that you can keep the business and home life separate and private. There is also less risk of cross infection via pet cats if the reception area is kept cat-

cooker of some type is required and a small freezer cabinet an advantage. A microwave is useful to warm foods which have been kept in the fridge (cats like food at room temperature).

Sufficient work surfaces should be easily cleanable and shelving and storage essential for the many and various types of food your guests will enjoy. Dry food should be kept in secure containers to prevent contamination by rodents or insects.

The installation of a dishwasher is an advantage in large catteries at very busy periods of the year. It is possibly one of the easiest ways of ensuring that food dishes etc. are sterilised between uses.

If medicine is to be stored in the kitchen it must be in a locked cabinet out of the reach of small children and must be clearly marked or refrigerated if necessary.

Stores

Storage units must be dry and secure and vermin free. Litter will soon be ruined by damp and beds and litter trays will need extra drying and disinfecting if taken from a store which has a condensation or dampness problem. Allow yourself

Above and above right: Different styles of reception
Right: Your reception area will be your customer's first impression of the cattery

free except when clients bring in cats in carriers. If space is limited the reception area and cat kitchen can be combined. In this instance it is suggested that the kitchen is positioned to the rear of the building with the reception area to the front, separated in some way with a barrier to prevent any risk of spread of disease or contamination of the kitchen. Only the proprietor and/or staff should have access to the kitchen area.

Staff facilities
Make toilet, washing, first aid and refreshment facilities available for all staff.

Work stations
Work stations are areas around the cattery which house litter and cleaning materials etc, which can be accessed easily and without walking the whole length of the cattery, and must be of sufficient number to allow staff to attend to cattery needs quickly and efficiently. They should be of a

large enough area to allow more than one person at a time to work unhindered and to ensure that the storage bins for clean and those for dirty litter and utensils never come into contact with one another. Stations must be under cover and as draught free as possible. Incorporation into safety passage is recommended for ease of construction and security. Construction should be as in the safety passage, with concrete base and wired, covered roof.

Isolation facilities
Exclusive facilities must be provided to isolate cats if infectious disease is suspected. These isolation units, as they are termed, should have a separate entrance and air supply. Construction requirements and standards should be the same as for the rest of the cattery. It is suggested that you have one isolation unit per 12 units. Because the equipment and clothing for dealing with cats in the isolation unit must be kept separate, facility for storage of these things in the unit would be useful. Isolation units should be built away from the main cattery but close enough that a careful eye can be kept on the cats inside. They must also be accessible and allow the cat housed there to hear and see some activity. Depression in a cat can soon worsen a sickness problem. An isolation unit should be built and erected in the same manner as the rest of the cattery, with its own safety passage and secure gates, along with an area for a separate work station.

Holding units
Holding units are used by many catteries and are considered by these to be essential for the smooth transfer of boarding cats. These units are used in cases where a cat will be collected later than arranged owing to delayed flights etc. or when an incoming cat owner is forced to deliver the animal earlier than arranged. The holding units create a 'crossover' pen. While this practice is preferred by many, FAB advises against the use of holding units. Many difficulties can arise in areas of cross-infection, disinfection and positioning. Holding units have to be disinfected in the same way as a cattery unit. Also, cats can become disoriented or distressed when held in confined areas or when moved frequently. This can lead to problems during their stay. If you opt to use holding units they must have solid floors and dimensions should be at least 1 m in each direction. They must also be as comfortable and as similar to full cattery layout as possible. Units must be easily and quickly disinfected. Holding units must never be sited in reception and must be at a distance from other boarded cats - it is difficult to know exactly where they should go! Cats in these units must never come into contact with other arrivals. They must have a litter tray, bed, food and water. More attention at planning stage to the possible need for a holding unit should demonstrate that efficient management will probably make it unnecessary. If, for example, you are building a cattery close to an airport, and you feel that 'crossover' could be frequent, it would be by far the best thing to install a full unit which is only ever used for this purpose and is not booked otherwise. A cat should never be left in a holding unit for more than 12 hours. See also page 68.

Above: Work station
Below: Isolation unit (left) separate from main cattery building

CHAPTER 6

Principles into practice
Cat accommodation

Wherever you decide to build your cattery and whatever materials you decide to use, getting the actual cat accommodation right is vital.

Components of cat accommodation

A boarded cat is accommodated in a 'unit' comprising sleeping accommodation and an individual exercise run. Each unit must have an enclosed sleeping area with an adjoining exercise run exclusive to that unit. An exercise run must not be used as a designated sleeping area. Communal exercise areas are not acceptable. The unit must have a securable door which opens into a safety corridor or area - a bit like an air lock to act as a catch for cats which manage to slip out of the unit door. Where units are accessed from an indoor corridor, doors between units should be solid, with a shatterproof observation panel to facilitate viewing of cats.

In semi-outdoor catteries the door to the internal corridor should be solid with a screening panel to allow cattery workers to view the cats.

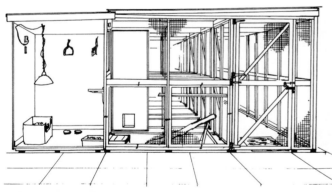

Above left: Full height sleeping accommodation **Right:** Penthouse sleeping accommodation

Top and above: Cross section of cat accommodation showing sleeping accommodation, run and safety corridor.

Sizes of cat accommodation
Sleeping accommodation

Overall minimum height of 1.8 metres with a floor area for the sleeping accommodation of at least $0.85m^2$ for one cat, $1.48m^2$ for up to 2 cats and $1.85m^2$ for up to four cats.

◆ These sizes apply in full height and penthouse accommodation.

◆ It is strongly recommended that the minimum floor area of any sleeping accommodation be $1.48m^2$ to allow for flexibility of usage. It is better to build single units to be able to take up to two cats as many owners do keep two. The smallest size unit laid out by the CIEH Model Licence conditions is for one cat only - which does not give great flexibility of use.

◆ All interior surfaces (including ceilings) should be durable, smooth and impervious. They should be easily cleanable and there should be no projections or rough sharp edges liable to cause injury.

Exercise run
◆ Cats do not go out for walks like dogs or use a communal exercise area. Therefore the unit must be big enough to allow them to exercise within it. Human access to the exercise run must be via a full height door from either the corridor or via the sleeping accommodation, depending on the cattery design. Cat access can be via the door or a cat flap.

◆ Overall minimum height of 1.8 m with a floor area of at least 1.7m^2 for one cat, 2.2m^2 for up to two cats and 2.8m^2 for up to four cats.
◆ These sizes apply in full height and penthouse accommodation.

Above and left: A cat flap will link the sleeping accommodation to the run **Below:** If a penthouse is used there must be a safe non-slip ramp leading down into the run

Most catteries use a proprietary cat flap. If a penthouse is used, there must be a safe non-slip ramp to allow the cat to walk down into the run. Whether this is straight or follows a zigzag path depends on the space available and the angle at which the ramp has to descend. While a young agile cat may be able to use it without a problem, thought must go into the design for an elderly, infirm, blind or physically disabled cat.

Top: View through cat exercise runs in an outdoor cattery **Above:** An example of family sized units which can take up to four cats each

◆ It is strongly recommended that the minimum floor area of the exercise run be 2.2m^2 (big enough for two cats) to allow for flexibility of usage. The smallest size run area laid out by the CIEH Model Licence Conditions is only for one cat - this does not lend itself to flexibility of use.
◆ In penthouse accommodation, exercise run measurements should be taken from the front of the sleeping accommodation as cats do not tend to use the area under the sleeping box if it is low (less than 0.9m high) - this then cuts down greatly on the exercise area they can have.

It is recommended that 10-20 per cent of units within a cattery cater for up to four cats from the same household - the 'family' units

Accessing the run
A cat flap at the bottom of the door between the sleeping accommodation and run will enable cats to go in and out as they please. It should be possible to lock this flap if required.

Lining and sealing
Fireproof thermal insulation must be incorporated into sleeping accommodation to combat extremes of temperature. Further to this, the sleeping area must be lined with materials which have a smooth surface and must extend to ceiling, walls and inner door. There are many different materials you can use - from painted hardboard to specialist linings - it all depends on what you want to spend and how long you want it to last for. All joints on ceilings and walls must be sealed to

Above: Fireproof thermal insulation should be incorporated into the sleeping accommodation

Left: Different approaches to flooring, showing lino and tiles and a smooth concrete run

avoid damp seeping into the insulation or the wood. Sealing must be floor to ceiling. While the use of strong adhesive tape is adequate, it is recommended that you investigate sealing with a plastic preparation and beading strips.

Where concrete or block and brick are used they must be properly sealed, smooth and impervious. These must also be resealed regularly.

Flooring

Floors need to be smooth and non-slip and capable of being easily cleaned and disinfected. Construction and maintenance must ensure that there is no pooling of liquids. The floor of the sleeping accommodation can be tiled, vinyl covered or a specialist floor finish paint can be used. Other specialist floorings can be considered – although these may be more expensive. It is wise to investigate several types (see appendix for manufacturers). It all comes down to a balance of cost/convenience/durability and efficacy of the product. Although cats are not hard on floors generally (unlike dogs in kennels where the flooring must be extremely tough), the surface does have to withstand constant washing and the occasional bit of scratching. It is important that the join between the wall and the floor is smooth and sealed so there can be no accumulation of dirt or debris. With certain materials this can be achieved by coving the floor onto the walls.

The flooring of the exercise run can be also be tiled or painted or simply left as smooth concrete.

Viewing window

A viewing window must be provided in the sleeping accommodation to allow the cat to see out and provide visual stimulation to combat boredom. This should be fixed and non-opening to avoid the possibility (although small) of cats becoming injured or stuck in an opening window.

Lighting

All areas of sleeping accommodation must be clearly visible at all times. During daylight hours this should ideally be

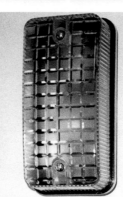

Above: A viewing window will be appreciated by residents!
Left: Bulkhead lights are useful in the cattery

natural light. During hours of darkness, or where natural light is insufficient, an artificial light source should be used. The switches for this lighting, must be on the outside of the unit with controls, leads, etc. well out of the cats' reach. One of the best lighting units for use in catteries is the bulkhead type. External switches must be weatherproof and it is strongly recommended that all electrical fittings are installed by a qualified professional.

Electrics

Sockets in sleeping accommodation should be out of reach of cats. Weatherproof sockets must be used if there is any risk of contact with water. Plan your electrical needs especially carefully and discuss them at the planning stage with a qualified electrician, who should then perform any installation. Cables must be fixed out of the reach of cats wherever possible, with armoured cables used in areas accessible to them. Waterproof sockets should be used where there is a risk of contact with water. There should be a residual current circuit breaker system on each block of cat accommodation units. All electrical installations and appliances must comply with heath and safety regulations, details of which are available from the local authority and should be well understood by any professional electrician.

Temperature

Sleeping accommodation must have an individual source of warmth. The ambient air the cat breathes in must be within a range of 15-26° C, despite external temperature. There should be a means of measuring and monitoring temperature. It is useful to have a maximum and minimum thermometer in the cattery as well as an ordinary thermometer - the max/min thermometer will indicate the highest and lowest temperatures which have been measured - thus it will show if the cattery got very cold during the night. A normal thermometer will only show what the temperature is at the time. Most good catteries will have individual thermostats on their heating system which ensure that the cats are kept warm if the temperature drops below a certain set level.

Heating

Heating facilities must at all times be completely safe for your boarded cats, humans and buildings. All controls must be out of the reach of cats and all heating appliances must be regularly maintained and checked by qualified professionals. There should be some form of thermostatic control to allow variation of heat depending on the environmental temperature and the needs of individual cats. Breeds such as Siamese or Rex, or old or ill cats may feel the cold and several cats sharing may snuggle down together and require less direct heat. Facilities should be arranged to enable the cat to be as near as is safe to its heat source, but also to be able to remove itself from the vicinity of this source. The cat may then position its body where it is most comfortable.
Open flame appliances must never be used.

Types of heating appliances

Infra-red lamps: The preferred type of heating, the infra-red heat lamp, can be positioned above the cat's bed but must be at least 1 m above it. These should be fitted with a safety chain which must be kept hooked out of the animals' reach along with the flex. Some types of infra-red heaters are fitted with a wire safety guard.

Left: Infra-red dull emitter lamp shown at a suitable height above the bed with safety chain and cover.
Below: Flush fitting panel or cassette heater in a uPVC penthouse cattery

Panel heaters: Depending on the design of your cattery you may find it preferable to use flush-fitting panel heaters or cassettes. They have easy to clean washable surfaces. There are different types and suppliers of this equipment: information on these is held in Appendix B.

Heated beds: Heated beds or pads can also provide heat. However, they should not be the only source of heat in an otherwise freezing unit. They are enjoyed by some cats where the ambient temperature is around 15°C anyway. Old or frail cats will be warm underneath but may be breathing very cold air. Cats may also be reluctant to get off the bed

Below: Penthouse style cat accommodation showing use of a heated pad.

for the entire stay if this is the only source of heat. Take care with the use of heated pads with pregnant cats - very hot radiators or pads are thought to have potential harmful effects on developing kittens.

Tubular heating: Tubular heating is another form of heating that can be considered for catteries.They can be floor or wall mounted horizontally. Waterproof heaters are advisable to cope with daily cleaning and disinfection routines. Do check that the heaters can provide the correct temperature for the type of cat accommodation you are building. Guards should be fitted to the heaters to prevent any risk of burning to the cats.

Other: Some catteries use a central heating system with radiators in each sleeping unit.

Cooling

Cattery units must have adequate ventilation for disease control and for the provision of airflow to cool the cattery during hot weather. Fans can be used during excessively hot periods, however they do merely re-circulate the air in the cattery. If a cattery is finding that it needs to use fans in only moderately warm weather, there is a problem with the design and it needs to be given a more fundamental rethink.

Shelving

Cats are a bit like birds - they enjoy the space they have in a vertical as well as horizontal aspect. They like to be up high - it gives them a good view and lets them rest feeling secure. Cats must have an external shelf for sitting on to view their surroundings and an internal one to sit on for their sleeping area window view. The shelves should be of smooth material, easily cleaned and disinfected. When planning your cattery, remember that you may have boarders (eg, disabled cats) who should not jump up onto shelves. Consider fitting some units with removable shelves.

Wiring, netting and fencing

All wire mesh used within a cattery must be strong, rigid and in good repair. It must remain escape-proof at all times.

Above: Shelving at different levels in the sleeping accommodation is also appreciated. Here also shown a panel heater. The brick work will need to be sealed for ease of cleaning.

Ensure that the mesh you use does not have any potentially dangerous sharp points or edges, especially if it has been cut. Square welded mesh is much better than chicken wire which can become loose and baggy. In the wooden cattery, mesh should be positioned on the inside of the framework of runs to prevent damage to uprights by cats scratching the wood. Any vulnerable edges where cats scratch can be covered with metal or plastic stripping (make sure there are no sharp edges to injur the cat). Mesh should extend over the top of the run under the roof and be attached firmly to

Above: Wire should extend over the run and corridor and roof to ensure that should the roof blow off in a storm, the cats cannot escape.
Left: An outdoor shelf provides a platform to watch the world go by.

the side panels (unless roofing is specifically designed and built not to lift off in heavy wind). Mesh must also be laid over the top of each unit between the joists and roofing material. Wire mesh must not be less than 1.60 mm in diameter (16 gauge welded mesh), excluding any covering. Mesh size must not exceed 2.5 cm. Some catteries may actually construct the entire run and safety corridor from solid metal and galvanised mesh panels, removing the requirement for a wooden skeleton for the mesh.

Sneeze barriers or gaps

It is imperative that cats from different households do not come into contact with each other and are not able to pass infection between them. It is not difficult to imagine how far a cat sneeze can project air-borne contaminants but these droplets are the best way for infection to spread. Apparently they can be sneezed about 1.2 m. There are two ways to prevent the spread of disease this way - gaps between cat units or physical barriers. A good ventilation system which ensures cats do not have a shared air supply will also contribute to the prevention of cross infection between cats.

Experience has shown that using good hygiene and husbandry techniques, a space of 0.6 m between cat units is sufficient so long as there is good air flow between them - gaps of 1.2 m between cat units would be prohibitive in terms of costs. However, it is only sufficient when backed-up by the strictest safety and cleaning routines. You will need a larger area of land to build a cattery with this clearance between units but you will have less barrier disinfection to do. Barrier gaps must not be used for storage as you may be introducing infection from a secondary source as well as reducing air flow.

If you don't have the space or don't want to use gaps as a way of minimising infection risk, you can use a physical

Left: Sneeze barriers between units – these can be permanent structures
Below: Sneeze barriers constructed of panels which can be clipped to the framework of the run and be removed for cleaning – here removable panels are shown at the end of a cattery.

Above: Cattery constructed with gaps between cat units

means of separating cat units. This is known as a 'sneeze barrier' and some part or all can be made of perspex/polycarbonate to allow cats to see each other and the outside world, while preventing them from coming into contact with one another. Because cats are excellent climbers they can and will climb up the mesh if given a chance, and can come nose to nose with each other if the barrier is not high enough. They can also sneeze down on the occupants of the adjacent unit. Therefore, a sneeze barrier will only work if it covers all but the smallest area at

the top of the unit run left for airflow. Barriers are best made of strong clear Perspex (mounted) in a well preserved wooden frame fixed into position over the cat unit dividing wire. These will be expensive to fit at first but will repay this investment by providing many years of use as barrier frames of this type are removable for cleaning and re-varnishing. Some catteries use a combination of approaches with two units together separated by a sneeze barrier in the middle and gaps between the next set of two units.

Safety corridor

There must be an escape-proof safety corridor protecting the exterior of each run door. The safety corridor must have a securable door. If possible, install an exit door (securable from the inside, lockable from the outside) at either end of your cattery to ease any necessary evacuation. In a cattery with outdoor runs, the safety corridor must be covered with wire mesh and roofed with an impermeable material. There must be adequate light in the safety corridor. Where natural light is not sufficient, again the use of weatherproof bulkhead lighting is recommended. In semi-outdoor catteries where units are accessed

Below: Safety corridor in an outdoor cattery

Above: It is wise to have a wide enough corridor to allow for people to pass each other or for disabled access.

from an indoor corridor, it is advisable to also have access to the accommodation from the run. A safety area of at least 0.6 m wide will also be required to prevent outdoor animals from having contact with the boarded cats.

The passage needs to be wide enough for someone to walk down comfortably carrying a cat basket and if several people are working in the cattery, for them to be able to pass

each other. Having too narrow a corridor may make working conditions difficult and annoying. A minimum width of 1.2 m is recommended for the corridor - this will also allow wheelchair access for disabled clients.

The safety passage should never be used as an exercise area for cats and no pet cats should be allowed to use it.

Protection from bad weather and excessive drafts in winter can be achieved by using removable barriers around the outside of the cattery – eg, along the outside of the corridor. These can be removed in warmer weather to promote the flow of air again.

Roofing

All outdoor runs should be roofed to protect the cats from the elements. The roofing needs to be waterproof but also filter UV light to protect cats vulnerable to sun burn and to provide some shade. It is recommended that in a wooden construction the run should also be roofed with wire mesh (under the plastic roof) as an added precaution against escape. Some lightweight roofing material may be prone to blowing off in high winds and may also become brittle and crack when aged – an escape risk which must not be taken lightly.

Extending the roof slightly over the front of the safety corridor can provide more shelter in exposed areas. There are different approaches to roofing materials and again cost can vary considerably.

Left: All outdoor runs should be roofed to protect the runs and the safety passage.
Below: Different types of roofing approach – on the left the main cattery building with open front and solid tiled roof and on the right family pens in wooden construction with corrugated plastic roof.

CHAPTER 7

Equipment for the cattery

Equipping your cattery will be a time consuming and costly business. Great care must be taken to ensure that sufficient equipment is available to control cross-infection. For example, you will need sufficient dustpan and brush sets to place one in each chalet and have spares to allow time for disinfection and to deal with occasional replacement. It is also well worth taking the time to plan the positioning of your equipment very carefully. Tools safely positioned and within easy reach will save a lot of effort. Listed below are basic cattery equipment requirements along with comments and advice. Local DIY chains are a useful source of cheap offers on items such as dustpans and brushes.

Beds and bedding
Beds and bedding which allow the cat to be comfortable and easily kept clean must be provided. They will also need to be easily disinfected and stored. Stackable plastic beds of a very simple design are by far the best buy. These must always be disinfected upon the cat's departure. Bedding will often be provided by owners but your cattery should stock small, washable synthetic quilts or pieces of Vetbed for lining beds. If condensation forms between the bed base and floor this is easily remedied by laying down sheets of paper. Bedding must also be thoroughly laundered between cats. Position beds out of draughts and (if using a lamp) below the heat lamp - with a clearance of at least 1 m. Where cats from the same household share a unit, a separate bed should be provided for each cat.

Litter and litter trays
Suitably sized litter trays which are easy to clean and disinfect must be provided at all times. Litter trays can be standard domestic trays. It is suggested that catteries keep in stock several domed or lidded litter trays since many cats will need them! It is preferable to use the same litter used by the cat's owner but, if economics dictate you will find most cats will adapt to a suitable proprietary brand. Please be careful which litter you use for long-haired cats. Dust and fibres of any sort stick to the coat will be bad for the cat and will increase your grooming chores! If using smaller trays, use one per cat. For groups of cats use a minimum of one larger tray per two cats.

Feeding and drinking dishes
Food and water vessels must be made of impermeable material and be easily cleaned and disinfected. Any damaged

Types of litter available include:
◆ Fuller's earth/clay - not best for use in cattery - difficult to remove from tray in small amounts, can be a pest with long-haired cats owing to its claylike and adhesive qualities.
◆ Wood pellets - good quality wood pellets are excellent for use with long and short-haired cats although you may find this expensive.
◆ Gravel type (Thomas) - easiest and most cost-effective of the proprietary brand litters, suitable for all cats, easy and economical to use.
◆ Wood shavings - a cheap method of providing cat litter but very messy, needs a lot of storage space, completely unsuitable for long-haired cats. Also, some cats are uncomfortable using it and some kittens enjoy it too much! Sawdust should not be used as it is too dusty. If wood shavings are obtained from a timber merchant you must ensure that they have not been treated with anything which may be toxic to cats.
◆ Newspaper - obviously the cheapest method of providing litter but generally not acceptable or familiar to the cat.

Tips: Investigate your local Cash & Carry for 'tote trays'. These make excellent litter trays! Look on the Internet for suppliers - you will find an enormous difference in the prices.

dishes should be removed. Disposable feeding dishes can be used. Water bowls must be cleaned and changed at least once a day. High-quality dishwashers are acceptable for use within catteries. Remember also to equip your cattery kitchen area with knives, forks, spoons, plastic jugs, protective covers, storage jars, cleaners, mixing bowls, etc, to assist you in the preparation and delivery of meals.

Toys and scratching posts
Facilities for play and scratching should be provided to allow natural behaviour and minimise boredom. Scratching posts can be purchased or substituted with logs. A favourite toy is a standard ping-pong ball.
TIP: Crushed ping pong balls can be revived by floating them in very hot water!

Unless brought in from home it is best not to allow toys made with sisal or fabric as they cannot be cleaned easily and can harbour infections. Be mindful of toys that are suspended from doors or hooks. Care should be taken to ensure that toys are disinfected upon departure of the cat.
TIP: A bored or unhappy cat can often be cheered up by a ball of lovely crinkly newspaper!

Cats love to sit up off the floor; if possible supply a child-size plastic garden chair or a wooden 'sit box' for positioning in runs.

Dustpan, brush and scoop

Each unit must be supplied with its own dustpan, brush and scoop. These items should be used exclusively in that unit until the departure of the cat and then be disinfected.

Carrying baskets

Your cattery should keep several carrying baskets disinfected and ready for use. This will make it possible to deal with emergency deliveries and collections - not to mention forgetful clients!

Storage bins

It is suggested that clean and dirty litter is stored and collected in bins big enough for a full day's use. These should be easily washable, with clean and dirty bins kept far apart. It may be an advantage to use bins with wheels and handles - this could cut down leg-work when daily cleaning and make rubbish disposal and litter refilling far easier. Some catteries are designed to incorporate bin bays so they can be spaced around the cattery.

Notices

Within the cattery notices should be posted with instructions on the following (see also Chapter 13):

◆ First aid procedures
◆ Fire precautions/action
◆ Sudden illness/death of cat
◆ General accidents
◆ Emergency help
◆ Name, address and telephone number of the establishment's veterinary surgery
◆ 'Do not touch the cats' signs on each unit

Your cattery licence must be displayed and current certificates for public liability, buildings insurance etc, must be easily available for inspection.

Hoses

Your cattery should be fitted with hosing to run the length of the cattery or with several water points where shorter hoses can be attached. The purchase of high-quality, reinforced and frost-proof hoses will prove a sound investment, as will the purchase of good, adjustable nozzles.

Bear in mind when positioning hoses that, in addition to a disinfection requirement, they are a fire-fighting tool. Hoses should be positioned where they are least likely to obstruct walkways.

Toolkit

Equip a cattery toolkit. Suggested contents: screwdrivers, light bulbs, replacement heat lamp filaments, spare security devices, cup hooks, bolts and wing-nuts, adhesive plastic sheet (for securing broken glass), fuses, petroleum jelly and working flashlights – they can be attached along the length of the structure with hooks to keep them up off the concrete.

Grooming equipment – see Chapter 14

First aid kit

A comprehensive first aid kit for staff must be easily accessible within the cattery. Information on contents can be found within this volume. A very good source of advice on and supply of first aid equipment is the St John Ambulance Brigade. They are always ready to invest time and effort and can supply some of the best equipment at very reasonable cost. Check your phone directory or the internet.

Please note: TCP and Dettol contain phenolic compounds which are toxic to cats.

Protective clothing

It is a good idea to have on the premises clothing which can help you to deal with a particularly vicious cat. If all attempts to befriend and calm the cat have failed it will still be necessary to give it proper care. It is therefore advisable to have strong leather gloves or gauntlets and a thick jacket, possibly leather, available for use when dealing with difficult boarders. It is important that this protective clothing is as subdued as possible and is put on away from the cat. While wearing protective gear one should move slowly and quietly and spend the minimum time in the cat's unit in order to alarm the cat as little as possible.

Security equipment

Purchase the highest quality padlocks, etc, and use in as many areas of the cattery as possible. Have spare keys in a place known only to yourself and two other trusted people.

It is well worth looking into the possibility of installing a modest security system on cattery premises. This will pay dividends in terms of security, and even more so in peace of mind.

Fire safety equipment

Suitable fire prevention arrangements must be made in compliance with health and safety regulations. Your county Fire Brigade headquarters will be happy to offer advice and to visit. Ensure that all fire extinguishers are checked at regular intervals and keep maintenance certificates to hand.

Position smoke alarms throughout the cattery. Your local fire prevention officer will suggest the number required for your cattery design.

Ensure that all staff are familiar with the operation of extinguishers and that they are kept in prominent positions. You must have a sound and practised emergency evacuation plan for staff and cats. Care must be taken to prevent the accumulation of any materials which may present a fire risk.

Transport

Vehicles used by the establishment for the transportation of cats must be properly insured, regularly serviced, kept clean and disinfected after each collection or delivery. Suitable baskets or containers for transportation of cats must be used at all times. Cats should not be left unattended in vehicles for more than a few minutes at a time. Consideration must be made for temperatures, weather, potential accidents and the temperament of the cat being transported. Have the telephone number of the client expecting the cat's return to hand and a mobile telephone with you. A traffic jam may be an irritation to you and the cat on board, but the delay that it causes may be a great worry to the client waiting at home.

Isolation facilities/barrier nursing equipment

Separate equipment must be used at all times in isolation situations. Brushes, buckets, etc, for use only in isolation should be housed close to the unit along with spray disinfectants and should be double disinfected upon the cat's departure. Barrier clothing, ie, disposable or washable boiler suit or washable shower-proof suit which includes foot cover is recommended. Before entering and leaving isolation units, carers must be careful to wash and disinfect hands. It is a good idea to purchase equipment for use in isolation in a different design or colour to other cattery items.

Holding units

See also pages 27 and 68

Miscellaneous equipment

◆ Sprays - you will need a supply of spray bottles for disinfectant etc. A good guide for purchase would be one spray per three chalets.

◆ Brushes - do purchase high quality scrubbing brushes - they wear out very quickly! Soft and hard brooms for cattery passages will need to be purchased along with deck scrub brushes for disinfection routines.

◆ Cloths - a good supply of strong 'knitted' type washable cloths will be needed. Check absorbency of these.

◆ Rubber gloves - a supply of rubber and disposable gloves must be kept for your use and that of your staff, most importantly in isolation.

◆ Buckets and dustbin liners - you will need a lot of buckets with strong handles and many, many bin liners!

◆ Paper towels and rolls - yards of paper towelling is used on a daily basis in a cattery. It is essential to keep a large stock of this. A cheaper alternative would be the installation of a free standing frame bearing large industrial rolls of absorbent paper.

CHAPTER 8

Principles of good cattery management

The designs and management ideas laid out in this manual are based on veterinary knowledge of disease control, ease of use, safety, and appreciation of what cats need in their environment (their happiness). This manual is written from the point of view of best practice for the keeping of cats. It will not try to outline every other aspect of management and business practice – these can be picked up from other standard business texts.

As in the design section, the basic principles of good cattery management are considered first. The following chapters lay out how these principles can be put into practice to ensure a safe and stress-free environment for the cats, giving them the best possible care.

Principles of good cattery management
- ◆ Responsibility and supervision
- ◆ Minimising the risk factors for cats
  - ● Risk of infectious disease
  - ● Risk of escape
  - ● Risk of physical harm
  - ● Risk of depresssion/stress/boredom
- ◆ Quality care of cats – see chapters 9 and 14
- ◆ Meticulous cleaning routines – see chapter 10
- ◆ Accurate recording – see chapters 9 and 11
- ◆ Training and standard operating procedures for staff – see chapter 13
- ◆ Recognising and dealing with ill or stressed cats – see chapters 17 – 20
- ◆ Knowing how to deal with clients – see chapter 16
- ◆ Maintenance of the cattery – see chapter 12
- ◆ Knowledge of cat health and behaviour – see chapters 17 - 20

Responsibility and supervision
Never forget that at all times responsibility for your business and for the much loved animals you are caring for lies with you. Learn to stay aware of the personal and financial consequences of running a poor cattery or letting efficiency slip. A boarding cattery must be attended by someone able to keep cats safe and secure and take responsibility for dealing with emergencies. A trusted colleague or staff member can be trained to stand in for you and will no doubt prove priceless - although a price can usually be put on a bonus and will go a long way!

You will be held accountable both emotionally and legally if a cat suffers unnecessarily or goes missing while in your care and the effects can be truly devastating – both personally and professionally.

It is essential that the proprietor lives as close as possible to the cattery to ensure that any problems are picked up and dealt with quickly and efficiently. This also provides good security for the cats. If not living on site the proprietor must be very close by and be able to get there within a few minutes. Good security systems and cameras can help with safety, however it is still really a 'must' to be on site.

Minimising the risk factors for cats
Risk of infectious disease
As anyone who has had a large number of cats in one place will know, the potential for serious disease problems escalates the more there are kept together. An animal's immune system can also be affected by any stress it is feeling so the cat may not be functioning at its best while it is at the cattery. Thus, a cattery needs excellent hygiene protocols to prevent spread of disease. (In this Manual this is also referred to as cross-infection.)

Cats are susceptible to a variety of diseases which can be passed from one cat to another. Successful spread of some, like feline leukaemia and feline immunodeficiency virus, need direct contact between the cats. Others, such as enteritis can be passed on via handling, or passed on by cats sneezing on one another, eg, cat flu. There is also danger of picking up disease from the environment, eg ringworm. Hence, the management of a good cattery must take these into account and try and miminise potential problems by:

- ◆ Having a vaccination policy for those diseases which can be prevented or minimised in this way
- ◆ Ensuring that cats from different households cannot have direct contact with each other
- ◆ Never have communal exercise areas - a cat should remain in its assigned unit for the duration of its stay
- ◆ Ensuring that cats from different households cannot sneeze on each other
- ◆ Ensuring that suitable hygiene precautions are taken between handling cats
- ◆ Taking suitable hygiene precautions to ensure that units are disinfected between cats
- ◆ Minimising movement of people through the cattery
- ◆ Taking prompt action if a cat seems unwell
- ◆ Making use of isolation facilities if required

Risk of escape

Every year there are reports in the press about owners going on holiday and returning to find the cattery has 'lost' their cat. A properly constructed and maintained cattery with good management protocols should find it virtually impossible to lose a cat. Some simple rules on opening doors will also help:

◆ The external door or gate to the safety corridor should be padlocked from outside when there is nobody in the cattery and well secured internally when it is in use.
◆ Anyone entering or leaving the cattery should look carefully along the safety passage before opening the external door
◆ Do not open the external door when any other person is opening a unit door.
◆ Check carefully on leaving any unit that the cat has not slipped past you and that the door bolt is firmly in place.

It does not take a cat long to bolt from its bed to the safety passage if it is determined to escape and/or explore. If it has managed to get into the safety passage the precautions above will ensure it gets no further.

Doors/access

Do not allow anyone through the main cattery door if it can be avoided. People quite naturally carry a lot of germs and are a great risk to security too! Owners must be allowed to settle their cats in and to say farewell but beyond this contact from outside must be kept to a minimum. Never allow staff to bring friends to work with them. Encourage all potential clients to visit your cattery but use this opportunity to point out that care is taken with access to the cats.

Risk of physical harm

Be mindful of the possibilities for a cat to come to harm. This is distressing and a very poor reflection on your management. As outlined in the construction sections, make all flaps, shelves, trays and bed surfaces smooth to prevent cats getting hurt when jumping or running around.

Some cats are rather athletic and keen on climbing the wire of the run. Collars, buckles or attachments to the collar such as magnets or identity discs, can get caught in the wire or on any projections, so do make sure potential problems are avoided. It is recommended that all collars are removed and stored with carriers or in a safe place, away from other cats and equipment (ensure each is labelled with the cat's name for return to owner on collection).

Although you will only have cats from the same household boarded together you must be prepared to separate them if they are known to cross swords or if the added stress of boarding frays tempers beyond normal. It is always dangerous to keep warring cats together - both for their health and for your reputation. An owner will always assume that the problem was more than just the cats' moods. You will often hear how they 'don't do that at home'. This is something to broach with any owner leaving cats together in one unit. Ask if they get on – many cats which share the same house do not always like each other. Part of your agreement should be that you can separate cats if there is a problem.

The obvious and best solution to all problems with potential physical harm, as with all other areas of cattery management, is to keeping a close eye on everything going on and checking boarders for any sign of any difficulty regularly.

Risk of depression or boredom

Any cat keeper can tell you that it does not take too much to make a cat bored or depressed. Cats are intelligent, active and social creatures who also have a great need for order. Who hasn't seen a change in their cat when preparing to move house or even when packing holiday suitcases? Changes to their daily lives can upset them easily and they are strongly attached to their home territories. It is therefore essential that the cattery environment is as calm and reassuring as possible. Encourage staff to chat to cats as they pass the units but discourage too much contact as this can worry and 'suffocate' the cat. Make sure toys and scratching posts are available and always check that the cat is warm enough and enjoying its food. If necessary, treat it to a different food (having previously discussed its normal and/or treat diet with the owner) and spend a little time sat in the unit with the cat. A depressed cat is harder to care for, more likely to become ill in your care and will certainly be seen to be unhappy by its owner on their return. A radio playing at low volume within your cattery is often a good idea for a few hours a day and it is always necessary to ensure all cats have an interesting view, perhaps across a garden or where the movement of staff and clients can be observed.

Quality care of the cats

An eye for detail in all aspects of cat care is also essential. From monitoring food eaten to noting a tiny change in behaviour – all will have an effect on the health of the cattery in general and each cat in particular. Chapters 9 and 14 outline some of this care.

Meticulous cleaning routines

As with care of the cats, ensuring that hygiene routines are maintained, from cleaning of units to washing hands, will keep risk of disease spread to an absolute minimum. Chapter 10 gives examples of such protocols.

Accurate recording

Accurate record keeping is essential to running a cattery efficiently and to make sure that all the information about the cats is readily available. Chapters 9 and 11 outline the administration required and suggest ways of recording details on the cats, their requirements, health and behaviour. Anticipating any potential problems and obtaining permission/contact details from owners in case of the cat becoming ill will also allow you to act decisively and efficiently if the need arises.

Training and standard operating procedures (SOPs) for staff

You may not be able to do everything yourself so the quality of your staff and how well you have trained them will be equally important to the smooth running of the cattery and health of the cats. Providing clear training and instructions will maintain standards in the cattery and help in dealing with any problems that occur. See Chapter 13.

Recognising and dealing with ill cats

The veterinary chapters in the manual (17 to 20) give guidance to what and how to deal with vet problems in the cattery, ideas on when to worry or when to act.

Knowing how to deal with clients

Chapter 16 deals with client care. Although a love of cats is the reason most people become boarding cattery proprietors, the cats do not arrive on their own - they bring their owners! No matter how good you are with cats, dealing well with people is vital to having a business. If you do it well you will have happy cats and clients and a full booking book.

Maintenance of the cattery

Maintenance may seem a rather boring subject but it is essential to a safe, secure and attractive property. Old catteries especially may have wire which has sagged a little or a small hole or roof which is not totally secure. A determined cat can make fast work of even a tiny way out. Chapter 12 outlines some areas which need checking and maintaining in order to keep the cattery standards high.

Knowledge of cat health and behaviour

By understanding how healthy/happy cats look and behave you can spot problems early. Chapters 17 - 20 outline many aspects of health and behaviour.

CHAPTER 9

Principles into practice
Quality care of cats

The construction chapters at the beginning of this manual explain the best methods of ensuring that housed cats are protected from diseases which can be spread between cats. These principles must be carried through in the management of the cattery. Anyone working with the cats must be aware of the disease risks in a cattery and the methods of management which will minimise these as much as possible. As outlined in the principles of management chapter, the risks of disease spreading can be minimised by ensuring that:

◆ Cats from different households cannot have direct contact with each other
◆ Boarded cats cannot have direct contact with outdoor cats
◆ You have a vaccination policy for those diseases which can be prevented or minimised
◆ You have accurate health information on the cat
◆ You have daily health records on the cat during its stay
◆ Hands are washed between handling cats
◆ Movement of people through the cattery is minimised
◆ Prompt action is taken if a cat seems unwell

This chapter outlines some of the routines and management procedures which ensure that cats are cared for correctly and are checked regularly while they are in the cattery. They also ensure that owners are aware of how their cat will be cared for and provide the information which is required for the proprietor to do his or her job properly.

Cat records
All cats booked into your cattery (see chapter 11) must have a file containing as much information as possible (cards/files can be adapted and/or cross referenced to cater for families with more than one cat). Collected information will be available as the cat returns for on-going stays. A cat in boarding very often behaves in an uncharacteristic way and may eat or behave differently to when at home and the information will give you a feel on how best to treat that cat when it comes to stay. Good records are also invaluable should there be a problem with a cat on its return home. If the proprietor can show that the cat has eaten and used its litter tray consistently and that no other problems have been noted then this will provide evidence if problems occur. Likewise if the cat needs medication during its stay, the

administration must be recorded accurately. Any strange behaviour or illness must be noted, and acted upon if necessary. Proprietors will also need consent from the owner to deal with veterinary care or use of medication should this arise during the cat's stay. Most proprietors build up an excellent relationship of trust with their clients, however, occasionally a difficult client does come along. On these rare occasions proprietors need to be able to back up their actions and show that everything has been done 'according to the book'. If you never have to experience an awkward client or illness or death of a cat, you are very lucky.

Quick access card
You may want to have a quick access card box which contains minimum information on the cat and its owner just as a quick reference. This could then refer to more extensive records to be kept on a computer or in a filing system.

The quick access card could simply hold the following information:

File on: GINGER OWEN
Owner's name and address
Cats name, sex and microchip number
Cat's age on date when first boarded
Owner's telephone, mobile phone and e-mail numbers and addresses at home
Name, address and telephone number of cat's own veterinary surgeon
Record of bookings and stays with you
Main file found under reference code . . .
(it is useful to use the cat's name followed by the surname of the owner to provide dual reference but file alphabetically under the owner's surname)

File information
For each cat it is then useful to have an A4 document folder to hold information on the cat's dietary and other requirements and to allow collection of relevant vaccination and health history each time it visits. In this way you have up-to-date information on the cat and you are not trying to add more information or change information on a small index card making the whole thing completely incomprehensible! The folder can be used to hold:
The menu and toilet charts recorded during the cat's visit in case the cat becomes ill on return home and you have to show how it behaved when in the cattery. These may help to show the cat's behaviour in the cattery, eg, it is normally quiet and doesn't eat until the second day.

Veterinary treatment authorisation form – this can be signed once and then filed in the folder – it does not have to be signed each time the cat visits (see below).

Current information form - completed prior to each visit to ensure the most up to date information on the cat's health and other requirements is available. This can be completed by the owners before coming to the cattery rather than try to complete them all during a busy day. They can either be sent back in advance or brought in when the cat is delivered. There are sensitive issues to be covered with the first time client, such as consent for veterinary treatment or what should be done in the event of the cat becoming seriously ill and these can be explained in a letter such as the one set out below or can be discussed directly when the client arrives.

Authorisation or consent is necessary in the unfortunate event that the cat develops an illness requiring veterinary attention or even if it just needs flea or worm treatment, while boarding in the cattery. In case of this eventuality, provision must be made such that the owner passes responsibility for the cat's care to the proprietor of the cattery (eg to give a flea or worm treatment) or to a named contact (such as a friend or relative) for decision making if it will not be possible to contact the owner directly while they are away. If the cat is elderly or has an illness for which it is currently being treated then, difficult as it may seem, it is sensible to discuss what should be done should the cat become very ill or even if it should die while at the cattery. These days cats are living longer – partly as a result of new treatments which are available for many illnesses, therefore cattery owners will be seeing more elderly cats. Most owners of these cats will be pleased that you have asked and that they can make their requests clear. For example, should the body be kept so that the owner can bury/cremate it? Talking to owners about these issues can be difficult at first, but gets easier as you become used to discussing them and, although death in a cattery is not a common problem, it does occur and you will be pleased that you have discussed the issues with the owner beforehand.

You may wish to put in a letter with your veterinary consent form to explain these issues to your clients together with a form to gather up-to-date information on the cat. The veterinary consent form only needs to be signed once. It can then be kept in the cat's file for any future visits. An example of a letter is given on the right:

Form to be completed each time the cat stays in the cattery

CURRENT INFORMATION ON YOUR CAT
Name of cat _____
Date of stay _____
Owner name _____
Home address _____
_____

Home telephone/mobile phone and e-mail address _____
Addresses while away – if available _____
_____

Telephone number while away - if available _____
Name of contact available to act on your behalf _____
Address and phone number of contact _____
_____

I have informed my contact about my cat's requirements while I am away   **Yes/No**

FEEDING AND OTHER REQUIREMENTS
Cat's preferred food during stay (including treats) _____
Requirements regarding bedding, cat litter, etc _____
Toys/grooming equipment to be brought in? _____
Special needs re grooming _____

HEALTH STATUS
Telephone number of cat's own vet _____
I have informed my vet that my cat is staying in the cattery   **Yes/No**
Give date and details of most recent vaccinations or booster _____

Please bring your vaccination record card with you - your cat will not be admitted without this being checked   **Card seen Yes/No**
Flea treatment used and date when last administered _____

Worming treatment used and date when last administered _____

Other current or recent medical treatment/illness which may be relevant _____

Name or type of medication, dosage amounts and regularity, availability of further supply if necessary _____

Signature _____

Consent for veterinary treatment
It is necessary to have authorisation from cat owners to arrange any veterinary treatment, administer any medication or parasite treatment and to arrange euthanasia where unavoidable. YOU MUST NOT PROCEED WITH ANY FORM OF TREATMENT EITHER PREVENTIVE OR CURATIVE WITHOUT THIS AUTHORISATION. (see Chapter 18)

Identification of units and cats
Keep units clearly marked with identifying numbers and with name-tags showing the current resident. Do not remove these name-tags until after the boarder has gone and the unit has been disinfected for next cat. This will save a lot of confusion!

A chart bearing information on the resident cat can be fixed to the outside of each unit if desired. This can be used to record eating and toilet habits for transference to your longer-term records (record/veterinary form file) on cat's

Authorisation for veterinary treatment

Owner's name _____

Owner's address _____

_____

Cat's name _____

I give permission for worm/flea treatment to be given if necessary
I agree that in the case of suspected illness, a veterinary surgeon may be contacted, my cat examined and investigations performed if required (eg, blood tests, X-rays).
I agree to the cattery administering any prescribed treatments the vet considers advisable.
I understand that the tests and treatment will be given at my own expense.
I also give consent for euthanasia should this be recommended on humane grounds by the veterinary surgeon caring for my cat, in consultation with my own veterinary surgeon and/or contact person. I have discussed the options for dealing with the cat with the cattery proprietor.

Signed _____

Date _____

Dear Client

Thank you for booking Ginger into Orchard boarding cattery. To help us to care for Ginger as well as possible, we need to ensure we have up to date information on his food and other requirements. We also need up to date information on his health and any special veterinary care he may need, and authorisation from you for veterinary treatment should he become ill. These days the administration of medicines, even flea and worm preparations from veterinary surgeons, requires permission from the cat's owner.

While this tightening up on legislation is good, it means that we have to ask our clients to consider all the possible problems which could arise while their cats are in our care. We now board many elderly cats and with this comes the increased risk of problems occurring when the cat is here. Occasionally too, a young cat can develop a serious illness and we need to be able to act in the best interests of the cat. For this reason we ask for details of your cat's vet and for you to complete the veterinary authorisation form enclosed. It may seem a little startling to be asked to give permission for veterinary care or even euthanasia – these things are rare, but it is better that we have asked you about your wishes and know what you want. Actions are not undertaken lightly - we will have contacted you if possible, and your named contact and your vererinary surgeon to guide us in the event of serious illness. The welfare of your cat is the most important factor.

You will not need to sign the authorisation each time Ginger stays with us – we will keep it in your file. Let us have any additional information you may feel will be useful or call to talk through anything which you find worrying. We look forward to seeing you and Ginger on May 16.

Best wishes etc

departure. This will be advantageous if records are kept on a computer as each series of information will be simple to update The information can be transferred to a single sheet filed with general record/vet file and added to/re-printed with each visit to avoid bulging files and yards of paper.

Preparing for a cat's arrival

In good time, preferably the early morning of the arrival day, prepare the unit for an in-coming boarder. Check that the unit is clean and dust/hair free. Make sure the heater is in place (if it is of the removable type which has been taken out to clean), there is a bed (owners may provide their own bedding), litter tray and contents, poop-scoop and fresh water and that the thermometer has been replaced after disinfection.

The unit will be very welcoming if it is pre-warmed, so give the heating a while to get to work with the unit doors closed. The temperature of the sleeping accommodation should be maintained within the range of 15 to 26°C. In winter this will require some form of heating (as outlined in Chapter 6). It is preferable if the heating can be thermostatically controlled so that changes are automatically put into action, for example in the case of very low temperatures at night. A maximum and minimum thermometer will allow monitoring of extremes of temperature to ensure the cat is kept within the acceptable range.

Don't forget to label the unit with the cat's name – if it is attractively presented this will be noticed by owners. Prepare the various record forms for behaviour/feeding/pee & poo charts etc to record the cat's stay.

Reception of cats

Make sure cats are kept in their baskets in the reception area – indeed cats should not be taken out of baskets at any time until they are safely inside the run with the door shut. It is preferable to take the cat, on arrival, directly to its unit, asking on the way if there are any problems with health, parasites etc. This way you will restrict the cat's contact with your cattery and its boarders before establishing it is safe to accept the cat and finding out crucial information on its state of health. If, for example, it has a bad case of fleas you can discuss eradication with the owner and solve the problem within a very short space of time.

In the unit, check the cat over yourself for obvious signs of any problem (see chapter 17). Do not overestimate what some cat owners know, or understand, or will admit to! If you are suspicious of anything, discuss this with the owner immediately.

Once the cat is settled you can return to the reception area and ensure that all the necessary paperwork is completed – this will include information and authorisation forms as already discussed. You must also discuss every problem - or potential problem you feel there may be - face to face.

Don't forget to double-check the owner's arrangements

for collection of the cat. Be sure you are both thinking of the same time on the same day of the week. Check the cat's current eating habits, any recent illness or treatment, contact arrangements and vaccination certificates. Gather as much as you can about the cat's current circumstances and behaviour. It just isn't possible to have too much information.

Do not allow staff or others to handle cats until you are happy to accept them and have placed them in the unit they will occupy.

Make sure you impress on the owner that you will need to know of any changes in their return/collection plans immediately.

Baskets and collars
Remove collars from cats on arrival. The exception to this would only be with two cats impossible to distinguish from each other. In this case it may be wise to keep one collared for a few days. However, if you do ever leave a collar on look very carefully at the unit the cat is going into for anything the collar could get caught on. It may be worth removing any 'dangly bits' such as name discs or bells so these cannot get caught in the wire mesh.

If the carrier is staying on your premises ensure it is clean and sprayed with disinfectant before storing. It is suggested that a separate area shelved and marked with unit numbers for identification be set aside for this storage.

Collars can be stored here too, after a disinfection spray. Do not allow carriers or collars to come into contact with any other equipment and remove them from the confines of the cattery as soon as possible after the cat's arrival.

A carrier can be left in unit if it is in the cat's interest. Although it is a little rare – some cats are actually attached to their travelling quarters and enjoy being in them! It must only stay in the unit occupied by the using cat.

Settling in
After a cat has been left it is a good idea to leave it alone for an hour or so. It can 'get its bearings' and explore its unit alone. The cat is more likely to remain calm if it is able to make its own judgments and assess its environment's 'pros and cons' alone.

Visit the cat after a while and - without handling it - try to make friends. Lower your body (crouch or sit on the stoop of the unit door) to a point where the cat can see you without having to look up. Do not look at the cat for long periods but make eye contact for a few moments often. Cats find blinking reassuring during eye contact. If the cat stares at you, look back at it a little but mostly look down – it will see you are not a threat. Speak softly and calmly to the cat – offering it a few biscuits if it is allowed them. Sit with the cat without 'pushing' it for a while and it will become accustomed to you. It will eventually approach you – this is much better than *your* touching *it*. Let the cat do the introducing. As you gain more experience you will be able to 'read' the cats and gauge the best approach. Make a point of spending a few extra moments with the cat again later – at supper feed round or when you close up at night.

Opening up in the morning
Cats need to be seen as early as possible in the morning. They need to be active as soon as they can and they need to see people and activity around them. Try to open up your cattery (which means opening any closed flaps and feeding breakfast) at least an hour before clients arrive in order to settle any unhappy cats and to make sure your cattery is tidy enough for visitors to see. This time also gives you an opportunity to administer any morning medication without interruption.

As a rule of thumb it is best to open up between 7 and 8 am. You may, of course, adopt a different time. Remember, however that if fed twice daily, the cats will appreciate the time for meals being evenly spaced. Your morning feed time will depend on your preferred evening meal timing.

Prepare the cat for the day ahead by giving it breakfast and fresh water. It is essential that fresh water is provided daily. It is perfectly acceptable to have breakfasts prepared in (although not earlier than the previous afternoon) if they have been stored carefully in a cool and insect free storage area – in summer they will need to be refrigerated.

Check that its tray is not 'off-putting' – this will be cleaned out during next 'round' (not long away) but remember that the cat would like to enjoy the smell as well as the taste of its breakfast!

Speak to the cat as brightly as you can and make sure it has no problems you need to deal with immediately.

Food handling and preparation
Food for cats in boarding must be prepared separately and away from home kitchens. The environment needs to be as clean as possible and access to the food area should be restricted to those who need to be there. Do not, for example, have staff coffee-making facilities alongside the food preparation area. Bowls and dishes (if not disposable type) must be washed using a dilution of disinfectant after each use. Dishwashers can sterilise and keep down lime-scale deposits - it is well worth investing in a good quality model for your cattery, although you must carefully research any powders (other than your usual cattery disinfectant) that you may like to use.

Food preparation must be undertaken as a separate task, not done in conjunction with any other cattery chore. Great care must be taken to ensure those preparing meals bring no outside germs to the preparation. Therefore they should change to fresh clothing and, of course, wash hands thoroughly. Utensils must be for cat use only and must be disinfected after use. Open but not empty cans of cat food should be decanted to a suitable, non-metallic storage container (preferably with an airtight seal, ie, Tuppaware) and be kept in a refrigerator for use within 24 hours.

Feed amounts according to the owner's instructions. They are certainly best placed to know what the cat will respond to. Get as much information from the owner as possible in order to have a variety of foods for the cat. If there are several cats in a unit give each a separate bowl (they may of course feed from each other's bowl but at least you have provided separate meals for them.

Feed twice a day - as close to 12 hours apart as possible and be ready to prepare and deliver small extra meals at odd times to nervous, elderly or young cats, or to cats with special needs. Check on the suitability of treats and milk drinks with owners. They can be very useful but can upset tummies that are unaccustomed to them.

Never forget to keep a cat supplied with fresh drinking water; water should be changed at least daily. Consider having a few heavy (metal or earthenware type) bowls for the 'little darlings' who have a need to 'go swimming'.

Household and boarded animals must never enter the kitchen area to ensure that there is no chance of cross-infection via food or feeding utensils.

Menu chart
It is obviously very important to plan the meals given to each individual cat carefully and to keep a note of its intake and preferences with each stay.

A weekly menu chart, with menu for the day decided and planned per day is an easy and straightforward way of recording what the cat was fed, whether it was enjoyed and how much of it was eaten.

Add incoming cats to your weekly menu sheet as they arrive and plan their meals from information on likes/dislikes, diet, medication and habit noted on your main record and veterinary cards/files.

After feeding leave food in unit until the next visit – note what has been eaten twice per day (on feeding breakfast and at last round at night the amount which has been eaten/left. Obviously a cat may be a little anxious or upset over the first day in the cattery but after this it is best to try other foods. Start with other varieties known to be given by owner followed by similar foods which are different enough to tempt. If by day three the cat is not eating try fresh chicken or fish and the usual 'tempters' such as marmite on bread and butter or a little soft cheese – just enough to get an appetite started. After this point contact the cat's own vet for further advice.

Whatever is fed or offered must always be recorded on your menu sheet for any future veterinary reference. At the end of a cats stay transfer all information to your record sheets.

The chart in our example is a suggested one. You may have opted for having an individual chart attached to each chalet. However, adapting any chart for these notes is a simple matter which you can easily 'make to measure'

Feeding rounds

Having established regular feeding times it is important that you aim to stick closely to them. This makes it easier for you to run your cattery efficiently; you will be able to gauge what time is available and your boarders will feel more secure and confident about you.

Feeding should be done separately to any other task. Never do cleaning of any kind while distributing food and NEVER come into contact with litter trays. Note what trays need attention and return to them, as a separate task, after ALL feeding and water replenishing has been finished.

Take time to have a few words with your guests at mealtime. They will appreciate a little company – especially when it is accompanied by food. Perhaps have a few 'treats' in your pocket to casually drop on your way out (if cat is allowed treats, of course!)

Be watchful of 'escapees' at this time. They will be keen to get to their food… but will also realise that you are expecting less mischief.

It's a good idea to have a trolley for your meal delivery. You can carry water with you for 'topping-up' and also a note pad and pen.

Don't forget that some cats (the very young or old for example) may have more than two meals a day. Prepare for the 'extras' in advance and be sure to also keep the delivery of these meals regular.

Plan administration of medication alongside feeding as far as you can but keep a separate timetable of medication needs along with your menus. It may help to get medicine ready at the same time as you pre-prepare meals. This does not apply to all medicine – be sure you understand the nature of the medication and precisely how and when to dose.

Where several cats are sharing a unit it can be difficult to know if each has had its fair share of the food or if someone else has had the lion's share and cleaned up all the dishes. If in any doubt that one cat is being pushed aside and not getting enough, then stay in the unit until you have seen all the cats eat or shut one of the cats into the sleeping accommodation to eat in peace while the other or others are outside in the run.

Toilet (pee and poo) chart

As with food, it is important that production of both urine and faeces be recorded. This information can be of real

Suggested menu chart

MENU	DATE am		DATE am		DATE am		DATE am		DATE am		DATE am		DATE am	
1 Jonsey	Ws	GoC	Ws	Fx	Fxff	Seb	Ws	Fresh	Iams	X				
2			Fred	JW	JW	JW	GoC	JW	JW	Gour	JW	Seb	JW	GoC
3														
4														
5														
6														
7 Basil	Fresh Fish x 2		Fresh Fish x 2		Fresh Fish x 2		Fresh Fish x 2		Fresh Fish x 2		X			
8 Topsy	Ws	Fx	Ws	Fx	Ws	KK	Fx	Ws	Ws	KK	Fx	Ws	KK	Ws
9														
10														
11 Tabby & Cleo	Iam L	L	X		Tibby	KK	Gour	KK	Seb	KK	Fx foil	KK	X	
12														
13														
14														
15 Emma	Wsing	IamsF	Wsing	IamsF	Wsing	IamsF	Wsing	IamsF	Wsing	IamsF	Wsing	IamsF	Wsing	IamsF
16														
17														
18														
19														
20 Jack & Jill	Ws	Fx	GoC	Art	Fx	KK	Ws	Fx	GoC	Art	Fx	KK	Go	Art

PRODUCE PERSONAL CODE TO INDICATE FOOD TYPE. Ie: FX(f)= Felix fish typ   **Highlight if not eaten**

TOILET		DATE		DATE		DATE		DATE		DATE		DATE		DATE	
		Ur	Fc	Ur	Fc	Ur	Fc	Ur	Fc	Ur	Fc	Ur	Fc	Ur	Fc
1	Jonsey	Y	Y	Y	N	Y	N	Y	Y	Y	N	Y	Y	Y	N
2				Fred	Y	Y	Y	Y	Y	Y	Y	Y	Y	Y	Y
3															
4								1 *yes* PER DAY PER CAT PER FUNCTION							
5								SEEK ADVICE OTHERWISE							
6															
7	Basil	Y	Y	Y	Y	Y	Y	Y	N	Y	N	Y	Y	Y	Y
8	Topsy	N	N	Y	Y	Y	Y	Y	Y	Y	Y	Y	Y	Y	Y
9															
10															
11	Tabby / Cleo	YY	YY	NY	NN	Tibby	N	N	N	N	N	Y	Y	Y	Y
12															
13															
14															
15	Emma	Y	Y	N	N	Y	Y	Y	N	Y	N	N	N	N	N
16															
17															
18															
19															
20	Jack & Jill	NN	YN	NY	NN	YY	YY	YY	YY	YY	YY	NY	NN	NY	NN

Example of a toilet chart. Ur = urine, Fe = faeces

assistance to veterinary surgeons should a problem arise. Record the passing of water and faeces on a daily basis as trays are emptied/cleaned and be sure to transfer the information to your record sheets/main file on the cat's departure.

Your toilet/loo/piddle and poo chart (whatever you wish to christen it) is also the ideal place to note any other concerns. Ask the staff to mark the chart if they find evidence of fleas, worms, vomit and other things you need to know about. This alerts everyone to the need for some extra care and/or action and records the occurrence for your files.

If a cat has not passed urine for two days it is time to become concerned. If you have any worries regarding toilet habits you must speak to the cat's veterinary surgeon.

The chart in our example is a suggested one. You may have opted for having an individual chart attached to each chalet. However, adapting any chart for these notes is a simple matter which you can easily 'make to measure'.

Medication record
If you are medicating a cat with pills/ointments/injections, administration should be recorded accurately and added to the cat's file at the end of its stay. See also page 68

Cats' comfort
Be sure to walk around your cattery many times during the day. You will need to check on all of the cats regularly and they will need to see activity. A radio is not out of the question – provided you do not have cats with you that are sick or will certainly not like it - it's a bit of company.

During the daily cleaning rounds and particularly during the last round of the day, have a general check on the cats' comfort. Make sure the heating in the units is working at a comfortable temperature and check the cats have cosy places to sit and sleep. If you close cats in at night, be sure to place any favourite toys, etc, in the unit with them.

Make sure the temperature inside the sleeping accommodation is suitable for the cat there. Each cat will have its own requirements; old cats require far more heat whereas two young and healthy cats sharing a unit will not require as much heat as a single cat. Some breeds, such as Siamese and Rex cats seem to feel the cold more than others and will benefit from some extra heat.

Check all cats for signs of illness or distress on a daily basis. Check the cats are comfortable and are not in need of grooming or flea/worm treatments.

Remember that each cat is very much an individual and has a very distinct personality. Try to get to know it well enough to judge what will make it happiest; remember that a little extra effort from you can make you both feel pretty good!

As we all know, under normal circumstances a cat will enjoy company and gentle handling. Be careful with new arrivals - it can take a day or two for them to become accustomed to you. Some make it very clear that they do not want your affection!

An owner is almost certain to be pleased if you can improve a cat's demeanour over its stay by paying it special attention. If you have time to spare, why not try some 'cat whispering' techniques?

Late rounds
The last round of the day should be at a time which is late enough to make cats comfortable for the whole night and for you to feel you have checked security well.

Walk through cattery checking all doors and locks and all electrical installations.

Visit each cat and ensure it is warm and well and has a clean litter tray. Double-check the bolts on units on your way out of each unit.

You may or may not decide to close cats in (close flaps)

overnight. If you do like to shut cats in, be mindful of the ones who may become very distressed. Ask the owner to decide if possible. If you have two-way flaps and there is little chance of serious heat loss, it may be nice for the cat to view the outside during the night or get away from his litter tray!

Carefully consider the security angle and bear in mind the age and personality of each cat as you decide. It may be more work but some cats will be happier 'open' while others prefer to be 'closed'. Experience will make this an easy judgement for you.

It is preferable to leave a little light available overnight. Rarely will reduced overnight lighting attract unwanted attention. A little will comfort the animals. It is quite possible for them to feel very isolated when away from home, in a small enclosure and in the dark for long periods. This is a matter of personal choice, of course, but experience has shown that a little pampering goes a long way – with clients as well as cats!

Remember that, above all, your late round is to ensure safety and security for your boarders and your cattery buildings. Never neglect this task, no matter how cold or wet it is.

Collection of cats
Prior to an owner arriving you should prepare their invoice; check the details of the cat's stay; collect up collars, toys and any other belongings. Have the cat's carrier ready (though not in the cattery). Greet owners if you can and remember all their names. Tell them voluntarily about the cat's stay. Explain in detail any news concerning sickness, flea/worm observations, feeding difficulties and any veterinary attention (make sure the owner understands that the vet the cat has seen, if it was not their own, will be happy to speak with them).

Try to deal with the invoice and any necessary discussions before entering the cattery. The cat and its owners will be anxious to be on their way once the cat has been 'basketed'.

Check the name of payer and payee, amount, date and figures on any cheque you are given. A small error is easily corrected at this point. Issue receipt for payment. Make sure your client has your telephone number/e-mail, etc, for re-booking. A compliment slip is a good way of giving a note of your number – or you could write or print it on customer invoices.

Take the owner into the cattery to collect their cat, hand them the carrier and allow them (unless it is obvious they would prefer not to) to approach the unit and call to the cat. Most owners and cats are thrilled to be re-united and enjoy the moment together. You can step in if needed and you will find an opportunity to switch off heating, etc, regardless of the owner taking momentary charge. Offer to help carry things to the car and express how much you enjoyed having the cat (even the wicked ones are good business!). Invite the owner to telephone you later if they have any questions and stay with him/her until they leave if possible.

Collect any outstanding notes on the cat for your record up-dates.

Clear the vacated unit ready for disinfection, disposing of any unfinished food etc.

Long-term boarding arrangements
From time to time a client will need to book a cat in with you for a long period of time. This needs careful handling. It is probable that your client is unhappy about leaving the cat and worried about his happiness. Be re-assuring from the start. Explain that cats in good care settle very well and that it is the habit of your cattery and all those within it to spare extra time and affection for long-term boarders.

Book the cat in as usual but try to ensure the owner visits if it is a first time client.

If you are running a good cattery this will go a long way towards allaying fears and will give you a chance to get a wealth of information about the cat's situation.

If it is at all possible (and later if not now) position the cat in a unit that has a bright outlook around as much activity as possible. The greatest enemy of the long-term cat is depression borne of boredom. Plenty of movement and people chatting to him as they often pass by will help a lot.

Invite the owner to telephone you as often as they wish to talk about the cat. If you can get an address for the owner from their nominated contact you could always send a post card to them from the cat – you will have a client for life and feel good too!

Cats taken ill in your care
If at any time you believe a cat to be a health risk to other boarders move it to your isolation unit as soon as possible, if it is safe to do so without causing pain.

Act immediately if you think a cat is in need of a vet's attention. If in doubt, ask for a visit straight away – the cost can be worried about later. Never waste time wondering. It is so much better to call a vet too often than to have failed on the one occasion you could have made the difference. Be prepared with all the notes you have on the cat when you call the vet.

If you suspect a cat has a problem, keep it as comfortable as you can without making it nervous. Spend time comforting and observing it.

As soon as you have enough information, get in touch with the owner or their contact and calmly explain the situation as concisely as possible. If you have called a vet other than the cat's own, speak with him as soon as possible too and ask them to confer. Also, make sure you are kept up to date with all developments, as you will need to pass information on to others. As soon as there is any good news or optimism, inform the owner and their contact.

Refusing a cat
In the event of an owner turning up with a cat which is obviously suffering from an illness which cannot be explained by the owner, the boarding cattery proprietor is faced with a difficult decision. The proprietor can refuse admission to the cat or can refuse admission pending veterinary advice, or accept the cat, isolate it and seek veterinary advice.

In making the decision, it is the cat which must be considered. If the owner is en route for the airport or cruise ship and the boarding cattery proprietor refuses admission to the cat, what action can the owner take? Thus, while the other cats in the cattery cannot be put at risk, very careful thought must be taken before refusing admission to a cat. If the proprietor does put it into isolation he or she must ensure that the owner is aware that they will be seeking veterinary advice and that the cost of this will be passed on to them – again the veterinary consent form must be completed.

Isolation
If you are at all worried that a cat may be suffering from an infectious disease such as cat flu or enteritis, it is best to remove the cat to the isolation unit to reduce any possibility of it passing the problem on to other cats. Infection is

passed on by droplet – ie, through sneezing and coughing or by fomite (equipment, hands or clothing contaminated by infected matter or body fluids). It is essential that all catteries have separate units, away from the main body of the cattery, used only for the isolation of cats believed to be a risk to other boarders. Employ barrier nursing – by keeping all equipment and clothing separate.

If you have placed a cat in isolation it is obviously going to need individual attention on your daily cleaning round. Leave the isolated cat until the end of the round so that it will only come into contact with you only after your 'cleaning up'. This will reduce the risk of carrying infection to other cats on your hands, clothes, shoes etc.

Isolation units must have a complete set of all tools and equipment for use only within their confines. All litter, disinfectant, brushes, cloths, litter trays and beds must be kept separate from main stock and used only in isolation. Protective clothing should be worn such as rubber gloves, wellingtons, overalls and aprons and removed before going back to the main cattery.

Use buckets and brushes of a different colour from usual (most cattery proprietors like to employ a 'red bucket' routine). Staff must spray feet, clothing and hands with cattery disinfectant at the usual dilution before entering and on leaving isolation areas. Keep stock of litter, etc, in the isolation area to a minimum.

Isolation units must be disinfected in the usual way. Ensure staff fully understand the need for diligence in this.

Make sure you check cats in the isolation unit frequently to ensure they are comfortable and secure.

In the extreme case where no isolation facilities are available or they are already in use, strict barrier nursing techniques should be used. Barrier nursing uses the same techniques as those used when a cat is in an isolation facility except that the cat is housed in its original pen. As a minimum this means that the cat should be handled after all other cats and:

◆ Separate food dishes, bedding, litter tray and utensils should be used
◆ The handler should change into protective clothing and wash hands before handling the cat
◆ Hand should be washed and protective clothing removed and left outside the cat's pen after handling.
◆ Shoes should be removed and changed for ones that stay with the affected car or dipped in disinfectant when entering and leaving
◆ Ideally a separate handler should deal with barrier nursed cats
◆ No visitors should be allowed in the area

Death of a cat

The death of a cat is the most difficult and unhappy situation you will ever need to deal with.

Be calm and understanding in all dealings with the animal's owners or contact and make sure you are armed with all the information they may require.

If the cat has been put to sleep it will have been on the advice of a vet and with the knowledge of the owner or their contact. Be sure to inform everyone of everything at each stage in the proceedings. Warn of the possibility of the loss in advance if you can. Encourage owners or contacts to speak directly to the vet concerned. If you are unable to speak to the owner of the cat, you will be dealing with a contact who will be reluctant to make the last decision and who will be

very upset. Offer to see them and to accompany them to the vet if that helps. Make a point of writing to the owners so that on their return they will immediately know what has happened. If you have carefully taken details of owners - and their whereabouts and contacts - it should never be necessary for you to break the news 'out of the blue'.

Follow up your concern and your efforts with a letter or card of condolence and be ready to support 'your' owner through their grief. It is a terrible thing to lose such a dear friend and they will see you as one who will understand – no doubt you are.

If you find a cat which has died unexpectedly without any obvious signs of illness, call your vet immediately and take his or her advice. The owners' contact and their own vet will decide to what degree it is necessary to investigate the death. Be doubly sure you have all your information about the cat up to date and be ready to give a report on its behaviour and state of health prior to death. Keeping detailed records is vital.

Seek advice from your vet and instructions from the owner or their contacts as to the storage/disposal of the animal. You should have pre-arranged instructions, but it is sensible and kind to make sure there is no change of mind. Take as much time and trouble as the owners need – it is rare for a cat to die in your care and you can do a lot to help its 'family'. See also page 69.

CHAPTER 10

Principles into practice
Meticulous cleaning

Any high quality cattery will tell you that it is attention to detail when it comes to cleaning and disinfection which is vital to preventing spread of disease, keeping the cattery looking (and smelling) immaculate and enabling them to pick up on any signs of illness in cats immediately. Most catteries find a routine which suits the way they work and ensures that quality is maintained. The following chapter gives examples of some routines which have been tried and tested and used to great success.

Cleaning and disinfection

A cat unit must be spotlessly clean before it can be disinfected. A good detergent can be used for daily cleaning and a suitable disinfectant used for thorough disinfection after a cat has departed. If a detergent is used for cleaning, it must be ascertained from the manufacturer that the disinfectant used to spray the premises after cleaning is compatible with the first substance used, otherwise the properties of the disinfectant may be rendered useless. It is pointless to apply or spray a disinfectant on a dirty surface.

Disinfection is the selective elimination of certain undesirable micro-organisms in order to prevent their transmission. It is necessary to prevent the spread of infectious diseases from one cat to another.

A number of different organisms can infect cats from protozoal infections, such as Giardia, to yeasts and fungi (such as ringworm), bacteria, mycoplasmas and viruses. Of these, viruses are considered to be the most important pathogens of cats. The viruses include the causes of cat flu (feline herpesvirus and feline calicivirus), feline parvovirus, (the cause of infectious enteritis), feline leukaemia virus, feline immunodeficiency virus and feline coronavirus.

The choice of disinfectant for use in a cattery is of vital importance. Because cats groom and are fastidious about removing substances from their coats and feet, they can ingest disinfectants. Cats are very vulnerable to poisoning because they cannot detoxify certain phenolic compounds found in some disinfectants. Phenols are found in disinfectants such as Dettol and TCP and are usually associated with disinfectants which turn milky in water. Cattery disinfectants need to be of low toxicity, without phenolic compounds, but be effective in the presence of organic material such as faeces. Disinfectants must always be used at the recommended dilution. They can actually become less effective if 'plenty' is used in preference to the recommended amount. Three disinfectants which are commonly and successfully used in catteries are Trigene (Medichem International), Virkon (Antec)

and GPC8 (Evans Vandoline International). See Appendix B for contact details.

Litter trays

Litter trays must be emptied and cleaned at least once a day and more frequently as necessary. Faeces which is allowed to 'hang around' will be a disease risk, encourage flies and not smell terribly good! Trays should be dealt with in a separate area, away from any food preparation. Some people let them air dry, slotted into pallets, crates or racks.

Daily clean

As soon as possible, but after at least one hour following breakfast, start the 'daily clean'.

◆ Sweep the run of the unit with the pan and brush stored there – tip sweepings into a bin or litter tray if it is to be changed. Include the underside of any outside furniture ('sit-boxes' for example) and the edges of unit fencing.

◆ Remove the tray from the unit.

◆ Examine the interior of the unit for any sign of fleas, vomitus, blood etc. – any warning signs. Note these down for full recording later and act on any worrying matters immediately.

◆ Make a note of any food remaining from the previous meal – this will help you battle any 'won't eat' problems you may encounter and will give you a good record of eating habits and any changes your vet may need to know about at a later stage.

◆ Clean the cat's bedding thoroughly. Brush away any hair on the cushions etc. and ensure the bed is clean and dry.

◆ Sweep the floor of the unit interior.

◆ If necessary, wash the floor of the interior - along with the bed - with the detergent/disinfectant of your choice. Be careful not to disturb any food not yet eaten. Include in this area the lower part of the unit walls, interior shelves, heat lamp exterior and any window that the cat may have sat against.

◆ Wipe over the exterior shelf – this is the last task.

◆ Take the litter tray to the work area and clean: spray with disinfectant, dry and re-fill.
Note the contents of the tray. Again, this information may prove invaluable if the cat's health becomes suspect.

◆ Replace the tray and settle the cat. This is an ideal time to have a little cuddle or a play with the cat, as it is a time of day when all things will seem pleasant to him.

◆ Wash your hands before moving on the next cat.

ALWAYS CLEAN UNITS FROM THE CLEANEST AND THE LEAST DISTURBED AREA TOWARD THE DIRTIEST.

For example: when washing the floor, wipe the area under the food bowls before the bed area and lastly work towards the litter tray.

ALWAYS PLACE THE CLEANING CLOTH BACK IN DISINFECTANT WATER AS SOON AS POSSIBLE AND CHANGE WATER VERY REGULARLY.

(Approximately every ten units)

Disinfection after departure of a cat

The most important part of protecting your cattery and its visitors is the preparation of a safe and hygienic unit.

The need for a full and detailed disinfection between boarders cannot be over emphasised.

Disinfects are not done every day of the year, and you will be very glad to get to a day without one!

However, it is important to look very carefully at the departure and disinfection routine at this point as it will be during/after the daily round that cats leave and the disinfects are done.

As with all other cattery work the disinfection routines are based on the need to clean units to a degree where there is no chance of cross-infection of any kind. The routine described here is based on a method which has been tried and tested over many years.

Be sure to study the detailed instructions for the disinfectant you are using and confer with the manufacturers if you have any doubt about dilutions. You may find that these are different in your disinfects to your daily cleaning routines.

Never use the same disinfectant water twice. Each unit must be cleaned with fresh solution.

Ensure the brushes and cloths you use for disinfections are good quality and themselves disinfected beforehand. Again – do not use these twice. Place them in a vessel to soak in disinfectant before the next use.

Never disinfect a unit while it is occupied. Obviously this is wasted effort, ineffective and potentially hazardous to the cat.

An experienced cattery 'disinfector' will take about 30 minutes to do one disinfect.

Try to fit disinfects into times of the day when you are unlikely to be interrupted. You will find you are less efficient if the 'choreography' and concentration are disturbed.

After a while you will find that, although they remain a real chore, you can do several disinfects almost on 'auto-pilot' without loss of efficiency. Don't despair – you really do get used to it!

This is the usual routine:

◆ Upon a cat's departure, unplug the heating (depending on the the type) and leave the unit door open.

◆ Return to the unit as soon as possible and remove the water bowl for sterilising. Remove the litter tray, poop-scoop and bed. Throw away any paper bedding and used food trays etc.

◆ Sweep the unit inside and out with the pan-and-brush set from the unit.

◆ The items from the unit – the bed, pan-and-brush set, poop-scoop and litter tray (once emptied) - can then be bleached/disinfected.

THE UNIT IS NOW READY TO DISINFECT

◆ Remove all furniture (ie, scratching post, sitting box) from the unit run.

◆ Pin back the unit door, remove the window (if not fixed) and the interior shelf and place safely in the run. Take the heater out of the unit (if it is not a fixed one) and place well away from water and walkway areas. Remove any other furniture – perhaps you use a thermometer in each unit.

◆ Ensure that all areas are properly swept. This will help you avoid cat hair spreading in the breeze and clogging drain-ways and will also help you have a smarter looking unit after disinfection. This is also a great time to brush away any cobwebs attached to the wire of your unit and its surrounding area.

◆ Prepare two buckets of hot water; one containing disinfectant solution plus a soft scrubbing brush and a clean cloth, the other containing clean water and another clean cloth. Collect a dry, clean, soft cloth and a spray bottle of disinfectant (at usual daily/tray spraying strength) and some paper to help you avoid stepping onto areas you have already disinfected.

◆ Using the cloth from the disinfectant bucket followed by the cloth from the fresh water bucket, wipe and rinse all accessible parts of heating unit. Put this back out of the way.

◆ Scrub the window, interior shelf, cat flap and all parts of the door (inside and out - including all edges and bolts etc). Pay particular attention to all areas of the cat flap. This is where the spores of ringworm are most likely to be found as the flap will have been in frequent and direct contact with the ridge of the cat's back. Wipe over - for best distribution of disinfectant - with the cloth from the solution bucket. Allow a few minutes for the disinfectant to work before rinsing. Rinse using the cloth from the fresh water bucket. Leave to air dry.

◆ Starting with the interior ceiling and then working your way round the interior walls (from cleanest area to dirtiest – or most likely contaminated) scrub all the interior of the unit except the floor. Wipe over - for best distribution of disinfectant - with the cloth from the solution bucket. Rinse with the cloth from the fresh water bucket. Allow a few minutes before rinsing.

◆ Scrub, wipe and rinse the floor as above. Remember to work from the cleanest area toward the dirtiest (obviously in this case it will be towards the litter tray area). Scrub and rinse any furniture from run.

AT THIS POINT YOU WILL NEED TO PROTECT THE FLOOR OF THE UNIT FROM FURTHER CONTACT WITH YOUR FOOTWEAR. It would be simple to re-introduce germs at this time. Clean paper will suffice if there is enough of it to truly cushion the unit floor.

◆ Using a spray containing daily-use solution disinfectant, spray all areas of the unit and all fittings in the same order as you have scrubbed them. Wipe with the clean dry soft cloth to ensure coverage.

◆ Re-fit the unit as usual – coming into contact with the fresh surfaces as little as possible.

◆ Remove the temporary protective floor cover. Close the unit up and turn your attention to the run. Spray all wood with daily solution and leave for a few minutes.

◆ Hose down the run very thoroughly, removing all debris from under the lower struts of the wire sides and hosing from front to back of the underside of the unit interior 'box'. Take the opportunity to hose around the outside of the unit (passage) and any other local area.

◆ Using a traditional deck scrubbing brush and after tipping on run floor about half a pint of disinfectant (solution as daily use) scrub the run well – including all edges as far as possible – and area outside run.

◆ Rinse the disinfectant from run floor with the hose. Open the unit door and replace the run furniture.

◆ The unit should be left to dry and air for at least two hours before being prepared for a new boarder. The optimum period is 12 hours.

To prepare for the next boarder, simply kit the unit out with the litter tray, pan and brush, poop-scoop, water bowl and bedding - according to individual needs. Switch the heating on and fill the water bowl an hour or two prior to the expected arrival.

Remember to remove the name card and other identification from the unit after the disinfect is complete. Collect any in-situ notes to add to your records.

A unit with no name card should always indicate it has been vacated and disinfected. Keep the safety passage well swept and clean.

Waste disposal

The Environmental Protection Act 1990 places a duty on employers to dispose of waste without harm to human health or environment. Depending on the type of litter you most regularly use - which will most likely depend on the prices - you may find several means of disposal. Some catteries still employ a burn-off method which works effectively but does involve an element of mess and possible pollution. All disposal is now regulated by local authorities who will differ according to locality. You must contact your authority as soon as you have you plans underway, or check current procedures if taking on an existing cattery. Much has changed in waste disposal legislation in recent years. Your local council will give you all the information you need, full details of their rulings and a choice of services and facilities offered to businesses. Most councils will regularly collect chemical/bio waste (as animal waste is classed) for a small fee. This is probably the most time efficient, risk-free and easy answer.

The Controlled Waste Regulations 1992 gives guidance on 'Safe Disposal of Clinical Waste' which includes the handling and disposal of dressings and excretions, medicines, needles and sharp instruments. Seek advice from the local Waste Regulation Authority or Environmental Agency.

CHAPTER 11

Principles into practice
Administration in the cattery

The vast majority of successful establishments are well-organised and well-administered. This is certainly true of boarding catteries. The more information a boarding cattery has on all of its clients, owners, suppliers, etc, the better it will run and the more able it will be to deal with all eventualities. Nevertheless it is also true that this information needs to be recorded and processed with the minimum amount of paperwork and paperwork storage possible. Beyond the legal requirement to keep financial records for five years it is simple to gather and maintain records without extensive or complicated systems.

It will be quite simple to maintain records on computer using the following examples as a guide to the setting up of charts etc. Daily updating from daybook and booking sheet (see below) is strongly recommended in this case. It is also very strongly suggested that copies of computer information be either kept on paper or backed up very regularly. There are now suppliers of programmes for catteries and suppliers of exclusive or pre-designed and formulated paperwork (see Appendix B).

Data Protection Act

As long as boarding catteries use the information they keep on their cats and clients only for advertising, marketing and public relations for their own business, they should be exempt from notification and other provisions of the Data Protection Act 1998. If none of your processing is carried out on a computer there is no requirement to notify. If you are at all worried you can find out more from the Information Commissioner (see Appendix A).

Licence

A copy of your current licence must be on display in your reception area or where it can be seen by the public. Current insurance certificates, FAB Listing Certificate and other such important notices can also be displayed.

Booking in a cat

The cattery booking sheet will prove the most vital piece of information you have. It will tell you which cats are in boarding, when they leave, what spaces you have available, when each unit is in use, which units are ready for a new boarder and which are not. On a daily basis it is the most referred to paperwork you have. Layout is important for your booking sheet as you will need to refer to it quickly for telephone bookings. The sheet must be clear and show unit numbers and dates.

Prepare sheets which cover one month at a time and keep 12 together on a clip board to cover advance bookings and full reference to all information. The example shows how simple the layout of a booking sheet is. They can be made in A3 size or as two pieces of A4 paper jointed. If opting for A4 it is still advisable to have both

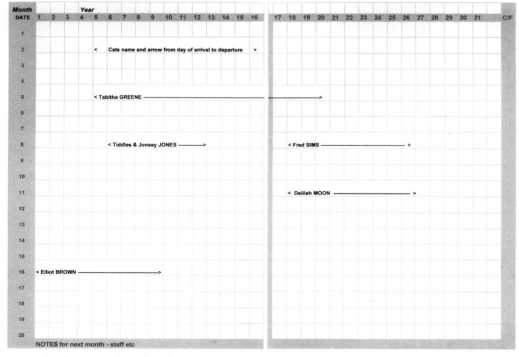

Example of a cattery booking sheet

sheets open on an A3 clip board. Protect your sheet from rain – you will probably carry it around with you a lot – phone calls come at all times and you will need the sheet constantly at your side to avoid the cost of ringing clients back.

Using the booking sheet is not difficult. Follow the dates of the required booking and simply establish whether there is an available unit for those inclusive dates.

If you are able to take the cat follow the little list below:

Existing client

1 Inform client of space available.
   Check client's name, address and telephone number
2 Check client remembers that they will need to:
   Provide evidence of current innoculations, give current information on the health of the cat and current contact name and address and verify the details of the cat's vet. Details of any medication will also be required (see Current Information Form on page 46).
   Agree to cancellation charge if applicable
3 Ask: If inoculations are up to date.
   Client to re-check day of week and date of required booking. Can client indicate time of day for delivery and collection of cat. Client to notify you as soon as possible if any change in cat or booking occurs.
4 Verify booking: Tell client they will receive compliments slip (and Current Information Form if you use one) as acceptance of booking.
5 Admin for new existing client: Pencil booking onto sheet – double check all dates. Make up record card with new booking dates.

New client

1 Inform client of space available. Take client's name, address and telephone number
2 Explain to client that they will need to:
   Provide evidence of current innoculations, contact name and address etc – all on the information form.
   Sign veterinary treatment authorisation form.
   Agree to cancellation charge if applicable.
   Agree to cattery rules as described in brochure to follow.
   Pay agreed amount on collection of cat (with deposit if desired)
   Transport the cat in a safe manner.
3 Ask: Cat's name, age, description, sex and neuter/spay status. If inoculations are up to date. Client to re-check day of week and date of required booking.
   Can client indicate time of day for delivery and collection of cat. What requirements will cat have for litter, bedding, food and medication. Client to notify you as soon as possible if any change in cat or booking occurs.
4 Verify booking: Tell client they will receive brochure with rules of cattery and map and an information form if you use one. Invite client to visit cattery in advance if they wish.
5 Admin for new client: Pencil booking onto sheet – double check all dates. Make up new record sheet and veterinary record form - add to files. Note confirmation on brochure and post to new client – write in dates booked.

Waiting lists

Sometimes it is impossible to take all cats wishing to board with you. This can happen during school holidays but is very likely over the Christmas period. Having suggested to your clients that they book any time over Christmas as soon as possible the only thing you can do is maintain a waiting list for your regular clients and a secondary one for potential new clients. Keep a daily eye on the booking sheet and address

any cancellations quickly. You will no doubt fill the gap easily. If you work with a good local cattery you can refer to each other.

Over Christmas clients would often rather take a reduced trip (to family for example) than none at all - give them a ring if you can offer something close to their original requirement – they may well be delighted.

Extras

There are many extra services you can provide through your cattery. If, for example, you find a really good deal of cat food or litter it is possible to sell this on to customers. Do not overstock in this instance – perhaps offer this as 'orders in advance' service. Some catteries sell food.

If you are a particularly good photographer or can make appealing cat cushions for example then these talents could add to your income.

Delivery and collection

It is a good idea to offer a collection and delivery service to your clients. Many of them may be incredibly busy moving house, short of time for getting away to a new grandchild, late for the airport or, of course, elderly or disabled. Set a reasonable amount to charge per mile (remember this can be reduced a little for the disabled or very regular clients). Add this amount to the final invoice showing the mileage you have done and the per mile charge.

Remember that this service will incur the work involved in the disinfection of your vehicle. It will be necessary to wash out and disinfect the area occupied by the cat and a good deal more of the surrounding area. This is possible with the help of disinfectant in spray form but must still be done with great care. Only ever use one area of your car for cat carriers and isolate this area as much as possible. Never transport a cat in a car not fully insured, MOT'd, and taxed – be responsible.

Transport the animal directly – never stop off to shop or otherwise.Check that the owner or another appointed person will be at the address ready to hand you the cat or take it back. Ensure the owner understands that the cat is transported at their risk – you may not be responsible for an accident that befalls you both.

Brochures

Make your brochure as attractive as possible. It is a masthead for your cattery. If you have a logo be sure it is bright and well positioned on your brochure. Do not overfill the space available but take care to list the best of the benefits you offer and include recommendations if you can. Use your brochure gently but firmly to list your rules of acceptance and make your charges and cancellation policy clear. Include a small map and directions – this will save you quite a lot of time on the phone!

Compliments slips

Keep compliment slips simple and clear. A small copy of your logo, name, address and telephone information is all that is needed. Your comp-slip will double as the perfect stationery for a short note (as per confirmation of booking for an existing client) if there is enough room allowed for at design stage.

Invoices

Invoices need to have an attractive but functional look. Incorporate your logo into the design and make sure all information necessary to contact you is clear. Two copies of an invoice should be produced – either by double printing if you use a computer or by having your printer produce self-copying invoice pages (this will prove much more expensive).

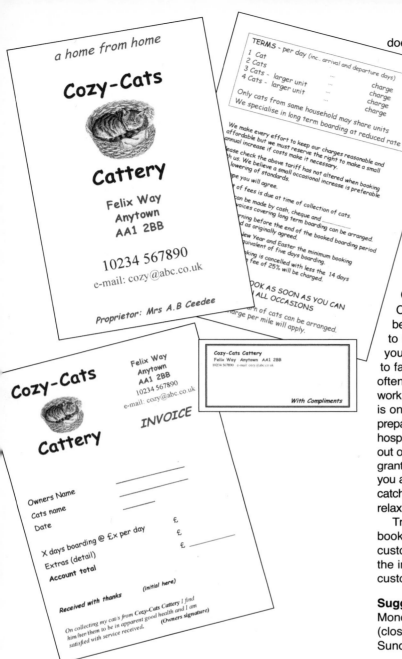

Invoice needs to show owner's name, cat's name, dates of stay – inclusive, daily charge, any extra charges, total amount due.

On receipt of payment mark the invoice with method of payment and with 'received with thanks', and your initials. Customer to retain one copy – it could well be from this copy that they find your telephone number when they wish to return! Keep all of your copies of invoices grouped by month to ensure smooth accounting and to enable you to do a little market research.

If your cattery is VAT registered you will need to quote your registration number on your invoices. Seek advice from your local Customs and Excise office.

Day book

A day book is one of the most useful pieces of equipment you can have - a large spiral bound book, A4 binder with a sheet of plain paper or an A4 1 day-per-page diary. For each day have a dated sheet noting every piece of information you may wish to refer to that day – both you and any staff. It doesn't need to be to detailed or even in your good handwriting.

Mark up your daybook the previous evening or as early as possible in the morning. List details of incoming/outgoing cats: which units are to be prepared for the following day: staff instructions and hours: notes or thoughts on menu: list of medication to be given: grooming details: expected visitors and deliveries: extra jobs to be done: appointments – and the other million things you may need to be reminded of!

Add information and details of the day as you go along and train staff to do the same. The more information the better, it will be easy to sift through later.

Transfer relevant information to your main files daily or weekly and carry forward any undone chores and information to the next day on the next day page.

Opening hours

Consider carefully the opening hours that you will set and be resolute in their application. Often you will be prepared to bend the rules a little in this area but most of the time if you adhere to them so will your customers. It is very easy to fall into the trap of being seen as open constantly and often what is convenient to customers (ie, before and after work hours) will be too inconvenient for you. Having said this it is only in the interest of fair play and good business to be prepared to make allowances for delayed flights, emergency hospital admissions, etc. Clients will appreciate your service out of hours when they need it but will soon come to take it for granted if you appear to see it as the norm. It is suggested that you allow yourself a reasonable break during the day for catching up on paperwork, making telephone calls and a little relaxation.

Try to arrange delivery and collection times at the point of booking. Make a point of clarifying these times with the customer when confirming the booking. This will emphasize the importance of this arrangement and encourage the customer to comply.

Suggested oppening hours
Monday - Saturday, 8.30 am - 6.00 pm
(closed 12.00 noon - 2.00 pm).
Sunday and Bank Holidays: 9.00 am - 12.00 noon.

It is more than reasonable for you to stay closed on Bank Holidays. If you decide to, you must make it clear to the customer at the time of booking that the cat will not be available for collection that day and that the booking must run over to the following day.

Be careful of Christmas season bookings. Many people will want only two or three days away and you can easily end up with many unprofitable short bookings and, worse still, a Christmas of disinfects! Consider having a minimum of five days charge over this period.

Make your opening times clear on signs, brochures, confirmation cards, etc. and ask customers to abide by them. There is no need to invite customers to ask for extension of hours, as they will no doubt request this if absolutely necessary.

If you have the intention of closing the cattery for a holiday period during the year make a point of informing your regular clients. The more confident of you a regular customer is the more likely it is that they will believe you will be able to 'fit their little cat in' at any time. A warning to a good client is a fair concession.

It is worth looking into having temporary management brought into your cattery during your holiday periods but you are strongly advised to investigate these 'cattery sitters' and check out references. Any fellow cattery owner who has employed sitters will gladly give you a report of them. Also consider training an existing staff member who you have faith in to stay at your home and keep everything under control. It may be worth keeping bookings to a minimum during breaks.

Payment methods

Decide on ways of payment acceptable to you - cash/cheque/credit card being recommended. Remember to specify which credit cards are OK. Depending on how you chose to run your business accounts this is nice and simple. Check with your bank or building society how many cheques you can pay in at one time. Remember that if you keep your books carefully and make notes on income and outgoings on a daily basis, a weekly assessment will be easy and your annual accounts will almost do themselves – saving you time and money (and anguish!). Careful keeping of records will usually make it possible for you to transfer cash payments to your petty cash accounts and provide you with 'odds and bods' money and often also wages cash.

Discuss with your bank the charges involved in accepting credit, debit or switch cards. These may be a disadvantage below a minimum amount.

If you wish to take booking via the internet/e-mail you will need to investigate security and payment methods separately.

When accepting a cheque you may wish to request a guarantee card but remember that many good customers will not have one. It may be worth taking a risk. The kind of person who wishes to take proper care of their cat is usually caring enough to want to be fair to you and to keep the 'next time' open.

A cheque needs to be looked at carefully – make sure the date is correct, the numbers and letters match, the name of the payee (you) is correct and that the cheque is signed. It makes life more simple to have a stamp made up with the payee name you want.

Always issue and initial a receipt to the customer. A good idea is to create a two-part invoice, one part of which is used as this receipt.

Non-payment

The area of non-payment is a very tricky one. It is however, a very rare occurrence. There is obviously no way you can take back care you have given to a cat boarding with you even if you wanted to. The following are practises which will minimise your exposure to risk of not getting paid and will ensure you don't get caught twice:

◆ Instigate a deposit system for first-time or all clients.
◆ Explain to clients when booking in a cat what payment is expected and when.
◆ Refuse a second booking if first is unpaid.
◆ Refer to local small claims court after three reminder letters have been sent and three months at least have passed. There is a minimum amount of debt to satisfy before this action can be taken. The clerk of your local county court will be very approachable for advice and information on this. Very often the threat of this action will do the trick.
◆ Set up a blacklisting agreement with other local catteries. Alert (informally) each other to non-payers.

◆ For first time bookings and non-payment, keep the cat(s) and their carriers until the owner pays up!

Staff diary

Keep a diary of staff attendance and performance. It will assist in calculating wages if staff are hourly paid. In this diary keep a check on who has holiday dates coming (remember - you can do a lot to help a staff member who has a family to cater for by being mindful of the need for specific time off) Also you will help yourself assess performance and spot any area where some assistance or extra training may be needed.

Book keeping

It is hoped that before beginning to keep your books you will have had professional financial advice and, if necessary, training. The right advice at the right time leads to a much easier life and a lot of money saved.

The system you adopt, be it manual or computerised will dictate the style you adopt for your accounts. Remember that you will need to submit annual accounts and that you will need to employ the services of an accountant for this event. It is a good tip to get this arranged well in advance and to discuss with the professional who will be overseeing your affairs the style of accounts most appropriate for you.

Do your books regularly. It is time consuming and difficult to sort out if left for over a month. Daily notes regarding petty cash and a weekly review and update of the book-keeping is the most straightforward way of keeping good order.Do not give any consideration to the option of customised/bespoke DIY financial software. They are almost always more trouble than they are worth and not robust. There are good, reliable software packages readily available off the shelf.

Petty cash

The best tip for petty cash control is once again regular notation of all in/out movement. Note against petty cash all the incidental items you purchase for the cattery – however small and obscure they may seem – and keep all receipts. File these in date order and group weekly. Any money outgoing from petty cash for casual labour etc. must be covered by a signed note of acceptance. If you use cash payments from clients to fund your petty cash/wages make sure you note this incoming cash in petty cash records and in your overall cattery books.

Client directory/address labels

Your quick reference card for your clients can contain any special information about them (ie, wheelchair bound, recently bereaved, etc) which will help in providing a sensitive and courteous service for them. A directory will make it easier to contact a client and can help you with the extra information without your putting possibly sensitive information onto your main record cards. If you are using a computer in your cattery it is also a good tip to list clients names and addresses on labels for postage of updated information, newsletters and cards.

Do send Christmas cards to your clients. It is one of the finest PR efforts you can make. Send to clients who have used the cattery during the previous two years.

Also consider sending a card to a client who has lost a cat. The bereavement felt is very strong and your support and sympathy will really be appreciated. A tasteful card or a short hand-written letter is ideal. FAB can supply cards if required.

Stock control

Keep a very careful record of the stock you use on a daily basis and all extras or unusual items (a specific cat food for one delicate boarder for example). Over the course of a year you will be able to judge your average stock needs and decide if special deals can be struck to save you money. Once a month go through your stock and see where you have run low and where you have more than enough. Careful recording of these actions will soon ensure you almost without effort have sufficient, well-balanced and properly rotated stock

A simple chart showing usage versus purchase will help you keep note of what you have in stock – even if it is stored in a back shed!

Enquire on booking a cat in if it has any change in diet or any special needs so that you have time to pick up any unusual requirements. Do not ask clients to bring any special needs with them, beyond that issued by a vet but do allow them to contribute if they wish. Many owners have a need to ensure you have 'some of puss' favourite' in stock and enjoy providing it. Accepting some of a cat's food from an owner does not lead to a need to discount their invoice but it may be reasonable on your part to do this if the food was very specific or if the owner bought a lot of it!

Directory of suppliers

Keep a current directory of your suppliers, service providers and available help. It will serve you better than a 'trudge' through old invoices! - plus you may need to get trusted or local assistance in a hurry. Note alongside each entry the dealings you have had with the individual/company, the date of last contact and a brief note on your opinion of their service and value for money. Remember that, as a client, you can build up a lot of useful goodwill if you remember to clear invoices in reasonable time, remain calm and understanding if problems arise and perhaps even remember the office staff (card) and delivery man (tip) at Christmas.

Holiday cover

Try to establish dates for staff holidays as early in the year as possible and be as understanding as you can regarding family ties. If you have more than one member of staff you may find they work things out at least as well as you do and can be left to 'stagger' time off. If you have weekend staff or young people in college for example, they will be invaluable during the summer months and possibly at Christmas time. A wall chart year calendar is very useful for marking up holidays, closures, events, etc.

Archives

You may be pleased in the future if you keep a short history of your cattery and its clients for future reference. Clients will appreciate your having a record of them if it has been some years since they used your cattery. Also it is possible that you may wish to write an account of your life in cat care (there will be plenty of wonderful anecdotes!) in your retirement. Keep a very short diary of the less imperative things if you can find time – if nothing else it will cause you much amusement a few years hence.

CHAPTER 12

Principles into practice
Order, security, insurance and maintenance

As with any business that is run well, there are best practice procedures which require effort but which will, ultimately, lead to a safe, productive and well run establishment. Within a cattery especially there are many such routines and procedures – the repetitive nature of some of them could lead to cutting corners or sloppiness which could be extremely detrimental to the health and welfare of the cats and ultimately to the business itself. There are daily cleaning routines, procedures for booking in cats, evening rounds to check on cats and yearly maintenance – all to be carried out to the highest possible standards. These are covered in previous chapters.

Keeping good order
Neat and tidy working practices ensure that things do not get misplaced or forgotten or if cleaning is not done well, then it will be obvious. All of these contribute to the smooth running of the cattery and thus the care of the cats. Of course, everyone has their own way of doing things which suits them and recommendations can be adapted; however, they do conform to the principles outlined earlier in this manual and will give the result that is required.

Work stations: Work stations must be treated as inner-cattery passages and cared for in the same way. You must avoid contact between containers for fresh litter/paper/water etc, and those for used materials. The larger the work station area the better. Remember that there may be more than one person using it at a time during busy periods. Food should at no time be housed in any work station and staff breaks should not be taken in their vicinity. Stations should be clean and tidy at all times and supplies replenished at the end of each cleaning round. A daily sweep and weekly hose down is essential. If a trolley is kept for delivery of meals/water it must be well away from all litter and waste.

Stations should be stocked with:
◆ At least one bin (clean) for each type of litter used
◆ At least one bin (used) for each type of litter used
◆ Paper towels
◆ Disinfectant sprays
◆ Note pads/charts for daily information and records
◆ Brooms and brushes for cleaning of passages (not to be used in units)
◆ Protective gloves
◆ First aid kit
◆ Mobile phone or intercom if assistance is not nearby

Kitchen: Keep the cat kitchen clean and tidy at all times and ensure surfaces are wiped over with cattery disinfectant each day after use. Sterilise utensils (a baby bottle unit would be ideal for this) if you prefer not to install dishwashers. If a dishwasher is installed it must be used only for cattery purposes.

Medicine cabinet: The cabinet must under no circumstances be used for any other purpose and medicines must not be stored anywhere else. Too many different storage places causes delay and risk of error in application of medication.

Stores: Chemicals must be stored separately in a designated area and if necessary locked away. Do not store toxic matter anywhere within the cattery and do not store medicines in any other place than a designated locked cabinet. Make sure you remember to create storage for foul weather clothing, spare cattery tools, a tool box, cleaning tools and all items which will be in the open under usual circumstances but need shielding from strong winds or ice. Make the tidying and cleaning of your stores a part of the daily/weekly work schedules, include them in your lighting/power point requirements and in your fire safety routines.

Reception: Keep paperwork relevant to each day in reception and have incoming and outgoing paperwork to hand. It is best to keep filing cabinet with details of all current boarders in reception in order to ensure information is always to hand. Make reception a comfortable and attractive place. Many proprietors have cork boards with photos of regular boarders and cartoons on display. Have seats available for customers who may be older or less mobile and those who take longer than usual to deliver/collect their cats.

Keep reception stocked with:
◆ Telephone extension
◆ Stationery
◆ Desk/surface for cheque writing etc
◆ Small lockable cash box (for change and security)
◆ Stamp for cheques
◆ Calendar
◆ Brochures and compliment slips
◆ Drinking water, tissues and other items customers may appreciate.

Staff facilities: Food and drink must not be taken inside cattery passages and smoking must be prohibited anywhere near the cattery building, ancillary units and everywhere that clients may be present. Proper non-smoking signs must be posted and observed. Many cattery proprietors find it is beneficial for morale and control to take breaks with staff. These breaks can be held in specifically created areas or even within the proprietors home with other members of the family. In this circumstance it is easy for the proprietor to keep aware of any news, problems etc and to maintain the friendly atmosphere they hope to achieve. Also, it is easier to ensure staff understand the need for hand washing after meals etc before returning to the cattery.

General: Keep all equipment in good order and replace regularly. Take time to occasionally (perhaps every three months) check brushes and bins for the need for scrubbing and disinfecting themselves. Keep paths to cattery clear and clean, particularly those where clients walk. Avoid accidents and irritations.

Safety passages: Safety passages must be kept clear of mess and cat hair. Daily sweeping and weekly hosing is recommended. As each cat departs and your standard disinfection routine is applied to the vacant chalet, the passage area directly outside and alongside each unit can be 'deck' scrubbed and hosed along with the unit run. Remove algae by regularly scrubbing with recommended disinfectant. This is far better done as the 'green' first appears rather than when there is a lot of it, as it really is a miserable job. Be very careful if tempted to use a chemical algae and mould remover. Many of these would be dangerous to animals. Contact the makers and carefully study chemical breakdown supplied by them. Safety passages must NEVER be used as exercise runs.

Under units: From time to time it is necessary to clean out underneath the sleeping accommodation of outdoor wooden catteries. This is a tedious task but, however carefully hosing is carried out, a certain amount of dirt and debris will collect and needs to be removed.

Landscaping: Driveways, paths and walkways within your cattery must be kept free of debris, algae and any other slippery or dangerous material. Gardens should be smart, clean and as impressive to clients as possible but, above all, consideration must be given to the environment/view of the boarded cats. A good idea is to plant some cat mint. It's a pretty plant and the occasional off-cut will be appreciated by many of your guests! During the summer months make sure your signs are not obscured by rapidly growing vegetation.

Security routines

Keep a diary or a daybook in which you can note a regular interval for checking of batteries in torches, efficiency of bolts and padlocks, light bulbs, fuses and sensors etc. Schedule regular checks of the heaters in the units. Have a good supply of batteries, fuses and bulbs etc. in stock.

Be careful to keep a locked cash box close at hand for payments, but:
◆ Keep it locked and keep key on your person all of the time.
◆ Don't keep it where it can be seen and be a temptation.
Always remember that the worst can happen, however unlikely. Be very mindful of security all of the time and remember you are thinking on behalf of every person on your premises. Develop a few basic rules for staff and yourself.

These are a few of the best:
◆ Deliberately look carefully down passages and walkways before opening any door in the cattery. Ensure there is not another door already open, perhaps someone is opening a run to start a daily clean at the same time you wish to enter the cattery. A cat can skip out of its run, down a passage and through a main gate in a second if it sees an escape route.
◆ Keep cattery keys on you at all times and lock main doors whenever the cattery will be empty for more than a short time.
◆ Tell all visitors and clients (particularly those bringing children) that it is not permitted to open run doors or to touch cats through wire.
◆ Train all those regularly in the cattery to have a specific alarm call for those occasions when a cat gets past you and out of its run. If this happens – and it certainly will – it can amount to a small diversion and sometimes even a temporary entertainment if the cat can get no further than the safety passage. Calling instantly to one another with a pre-agreed call will prevent an outside door being opened unwittingly while you are coaxing an 'Houdini' back into its unit.
◆ Calls of 'overboard', 'escape' and 'alert, alert' have been heard! Just make sure you all use the same one.

Treating timber
For wooden catteries or catteries with wood incorported in runs etc, wooden exteriors must be treated regularly with a wood preservative. Creosote is toxic to cats and should not be used. Cuprinol has been used successfully in many catteries. It must be emphasised that cats must not be allowed near or to come into contact with any structure being treated with preservative until the surface is completely dry.

Maintenance
Do a 'maintenance round' approximately every three months with a notebook and list any minor repairs, improvements and smartening up tasks you need to do. Perhaps you could set aside a specific time each week for attending to these things. It is always better to do a little light maintenance regularly; otherwise you can end up with far too much to cope with all at once, perhaps at a busy time or in rotten weather.

It is recommended that each spring you take a very long look at your cattery, ancillary buildings and equipment and create a maintenance plan for the coming 12 months. This will enable you to arrange work to be done when your cattery is less busy (remember heavy work can cause noise and dust pollution and disturbance to cats) and when the weather is appropriate. A long-term maintenance plan will also give you time to spread the cost or workload of projects and time to order any equipment you need in place well in advance. Nobody wants to find they forgot to ensure they had enough decent litter trays in stock for Christmas!

It would be worth creating a 'maintenance calendar'. Over a few years you will be able to judge which jobs are done most regularly, which must be done at a particular time of year, which are most time consuming, most expensive and those you can file under DIY. This will allow you to plan a long way ahead. Barring the unexpected, this should save a lot of time, energy and money.

Fire precautions
The likelihood of fire in an outdoor cattery is extremely remote. It is prudent, however, not only to have all electrics

professionally installed but also to have them professionally inspected and tested regularly. A hose may already run the full length of the cattery in outdoor catteries and approved fire extinguishers should be strategically positioned. These extinguishers must be inspected and serviced regulary by a fire extinguisher service. See also page 69.

Insurances

The best advice that can be given to either the new or experienced cattery proprietor on insurance matters is to have a consultation (preferably as recommended by your financial advisor) with an independent insurance broker. Much depends on the type of insurance you need, what areas of your cattery and/or home you wish to include and the area you live and trade in.

The area of insurance is complicated and it is by far the best thing to seek the best advice. It is possible to save an enormous amount of money, not to mention worry, by dealing directly with an established expert.

You will need to look into building, cat loss, staff insurance, public liability etc. Make a full list of all you wish to discuss insuring before visiting a professional. Ask if there will be advantages if including your personal insurance. There may be a benefit in purchasing a 'package deal'

Review your insurance arrangements regularly. The ever-shifting trends of modern business can affect financial matters very quickly.

The question of insurance of cats in boarding is another complex one. Many catteries no longer purchase 'blanket' insurance as it seems to prove expensive in the long term and most cats are now covered by owners' insurance policies. It must be clearly established and understood on booking a cat into your cattery that its veterinary care is covered by its owner either by their own insurance of by virtue of the agreement they make with you when signing the veterinary treatment authorisation form.

CHAPTER 13

Principles into practice
Standard operating procedures

It is most important to have a set of clear instructions for your cattery so that everyone knows how to approach a certain task or how to deal with an emergency (often referred to as SOPs – standard operating procedures). These must be given to staff so they are aware of how the cattery works. Even if you only occasionally have staff in to help, just putting the information together can be a very useful way of making sure you have thought everything through yourself and are prepared. If you were ill and someone had to come in and help for a period, all of this would already be in place. If you have staff they need to be aware of this information. SOPs are excellent to use for training new staff or temporary staff.

Putting together a serious set of cattery instructions is not as dramatic as it may at first seem. They will give you a firm hold on the behaviour of others who will become very familiar with your views and will help you to judge and deal with problems as they occur. A firm instruction on holding units, for example, will make it easier for you to decide if a procedure you encounter (or which you are considering) is acceptable – within or outside your 'fine lines' so to speak.

Prepare written instructions and make them available for staff and clients to see. This will keep your policies clear in your staff's mind as well as your own. It will also tell clients what you expect and what they can rely on from you.

These can include procedures for booking in, for cleaning, for holding units, collars, illness or death of a cat, fire, escape of a cat and anything where you feel you need to have a set procedure, approach to a problem or task, or to put down a marker for quality or communication which staff can then follow.

Previous chapters outline in detail things like cleaning procedures so these will not be covered again here. Below are some suggestions of how to approach certain topics and the kind of information you need to provide. You may have others you wish to add to these.

Before putting your SOPs into use, give them to someone to read and try out. Make sure instructions are clear and nothing has been left out.

Escape of a cat
The FAB Standard for Construction and Management of Catteries and the Model Licence Conditions and Guidance for Cat Boarding Establishments, both insist that cat units must open onto secure corridors or other secure areas so that cats are not able to escape

from the premises. Of course the fact that there are doors which can be open means there is potential for cats to escape if everyone is not aware of the safety protocols. Things to include in your SOP:

◆ Prevention is always better than cure
  ● Keep the safety passage door locked at all times while working in the cattery.
  ● Use a door bell for visitors and staff to gain attention.
  ● Lock the safety gate at all times.
◆ Ensure that there is sufficient lighting in the safety corridor and external security lighting in order to see in dark or winter conditions.
◆ Should a cat escape it is essential to have a pre-prepared protocol that all staff are fully aware of and in which they are regularly trained. For example:
  ● Keep calm
  ● Secure unit door to prevent other cats from escaping.
  ● Secure all external doors.
  ● Call the cat by name.
  ● Place favourite food in cat trap and put in appropriate area.
  ● Inform neighbours, local veterinary surgery, local rescue organisations, shops, library and local council.
  ● Inform local press and radio.
  ● Inform owner's neighbours to look out for cat, should it return home.
  ● Contact owner or family/friend.
  ● Offer reward for return of cat.
  ● Contact insurance company/agent.

You must find the cat and return it to safety. If you do not you must be able to show the owner that it was a very very rare occurrence and that steps are in place to prevent it ever happening again. You must also be able to show the owner that you have made every attempt to find the cat. Asking them to pay is of course out of the question!

Illness in a cat
If a cat is suspected of being ill or injured:
◆ A veterinary surgeon must be contacted for advice immediately.
◆ Any instructions for treatment must be strictly followed.
◆ Any medication must be used only for the cat for which it is prescribed.
◆ A medication record sheet must be kept for each cat.
◆ The proprietor must obtain each owner's permission for the use of, or potential use of any prescription only medicine.

- All medicines must be stored in accordance with the manufacturers' instructions.

It is considered good practice to have a pre-prepared card to record accurately the owner's name, name of the cat, time and frequency medication is to be given and the signature of the person administering the medication (see below). See chapters 17 and 18.

Sample Medication Chart

Owner's name ....

Cat's name ....

Medication ....

Method of administration of medicine ....

Frequency ....

Expiry date of medicine ....

Date................. Time administered ....

Signature ....

Notes ....

....

....

Use of holding units

This topic is covered on page 27. If it is necessary to use holding units all staff should know where it is to be sited, how and when to disinfect and if it is planned that a cat is to be held. The following is a suitable SOP.

- A holding unit should be used only in an emergency. A cat should not be kept any longer than is absolutely necessary within the holding unit.
- A cat should not be kept in a holding unit for more than 12 hours.
- A cat in a holding unit must be provided with a bed, litter tray, food and water.
- Record accurately details of admission into a holding unit.
- An owner should always be informed of intention to place a cat into the holding unit.
- A signature should be obtained from the owner or owner's representative or contact giving permission to move the cat from the chalet into the holding unit.

Collars

This topic is covered on on page 48. Suggested inclusion in your SOP:

- On admission remove collars.
- Where collars have attached cat flap keys or magnets, give the collar to the owner to take home so that the collar can be put on the cat on it's return (or brought back when they pick the cat up).
- Collars retained at the cattery should be placed into a plastic bag, clearly marked with owner's name, cat's name, date of arrival and departure date. (Alternatively a freezer bag can be used and the details written straight onto the bag).
- Keep in a secure area and give to the owner prior to departure.
  (Do not forget to give collars back, especially to latch key cats!)

Death of a cat

Sample holding unit checklist

Owner ....

Cat's name...

Health check .... date.................time..........

Date.............. time .... of agreed collection/delivery

Informed of reason for delay by owner .... yes / no

Family/friend contacted to inform of arrangement for holding until new agreed collection time .... yes / no

Date .... time .... cat removed from holding unit

Condition of cat on removal from holding unit

....

Signature of owner ....
(if planned use of holding unit)

This topic is covered on page 52. When a cat has died on the premises:

- Advice must be sought immediately from the cattery's veterinary surgeon.
- A written record must be kept and the owner or owner's contact notified as soon as possible.
- The body should be dealt with in accordance with advice from the cattery's veterinary surgeon and the owner's consent form.
- Detailed records must be kept regarding the events leading up and immediately after the cat has died.

Fire

Sample form

Owner's name ....

Cat's name ....

Date .... Time .... of death

Owner notified .... yes/no   date .... time......
Family/friend notified....... yes/no   date .... time .....

A statement from the veterinary surgeon to confirm the cause of death, if known and that there is no obvious sign of harm or injury to cat.

Yes/No ....

Cat's current resting place
....

Owners instructions regarding dealing with the body complied with? Yes/No ....

Veterinary fees ....
Insurance informed Yes/No ....

Veterinary surgeons's signature ....

Proprietor's signature ....

Date .... Time ....

The Pet Animals Act, 1951 states that 'appropriate steps will be taken in cases of fire or other emergency'

That is the extent of the law relating to catteries and other licensed animal establishments. However, it is necessary to have an agreed protocol for dealing with a fire that staff are aware of and in which they are regularly trained .

Each cattery is required to draw up their own instructions depending on their own specific requirements. Free fire safety advice can be obtained by contacting your local Fire Safety Officer.

Adequate precautions must be taken to prevent and combat fire.

Fire safety booklet

A cattery fire safety booklet is an excellent idea. It is intended to assist you and staff in preventing an outbreak of fire, or if a fire should occur, will assist you in preventing injury and unnecessary damage to premises. The following list is not exhaustive and can be amended to suit individual cattery needs. Your Fire Safety Officer will advise.

Useful phone numbers: Community Fire Safety, Fire Service Headquarters, Local Fire Safety District Officer
IN EMERGENCY DIAL 999

Means of escape: Ensure that you
◆ Keep corridors clear of storage and waste material
◆ Keep areas outside of exit doors clear of obstructions at all times
◆ Indicate clearly exits and access areas which are not in normal use, with the exit signs visible from the furthermost part of a room.

Fire alarm: Ensure that the fire alarm system is in working order, that the staff knows how to use it and what action must be taken on hearing the alarm.

Fire extinguishers/hose reels: Fire extinguishers and hose reels are intended for fires in the early stages. All staff must know where extinguishers are sited and how to operate them safely.

Emergency and general lighting: Ensure that all lighting systems are checked and maintained regularly. Replace any defective bulbs/tubes/components immediately.
Due to the possibility of a failure of the normal lighting supply, a backup must be available (a good quality, strong re-chargeable torch, checked regularly is a useful tool to have available in the cattery and office).

Fire fighting equipment: It is recommended that regular inspection of all extinguishers and equipment should be carried out. This is to make sure that the appliances are in their proper position and have not been discharged, or lost pressure, or suffered obvious damage. The frequency of the inspection should be not less than every four months but preferably monthly. The proprietor should also ensure that extinguishers and equipment are serviced and maintained as recommended in current British Standards.

Be aware of common fire causes:

◆ *Electricity:* It is a source of heat. Faults should be repaired immediately by a competent electrician. Switch off appliances after use. Old wiring should be regularly checked and renewed if necessary. You may need extra ring circuits to cope with increasing numbers of electrical appliances.
Heating: Keep portable heating appliances away from any combustible material.
◆ *Rubbish:* remove rubbish from the premises and into bins with lids as quickly and as often as possible.
◆ *Smoking:* A very frequent fire starter. Never allow smoking in the vicinity of the cattery.
◆ *Dangerous Goods:* Keep aerosols and other dangerous substances away from any heat source to maintain a safe working environment.
◆ *Arson:* Help to protect your premises from the arsonist by locking away any flammable substances. Secure the cattery premises at the end of the day.

WHAT TO DO IN CASE OF FIRE

If a fire alarm is raised, the staff and cats must be evacuated following your prepared evacuation plan. This will relate specifically to the design of your cattery.

When leaving the building do everything possible to help reduce the possibility of the fire spreading.

Ensure that the fire brigade is called immediately and that a responsible person is designated to meet the fire appliance when it arrives.

Do not re-enter the premises for any reason.

Instructions to staff: Ensure that all staff are aware of their responsibilities in the event of an emergency. Ensure that they know:
◆ How to raise the alarm
◆ How to call for the fire brigade
◆ When not to tackle a fire
◆ How to use a fire extinguisher correctly and safely
◆The correct evacuation procedure for the cattery

Instruction should be given in respect of the following:-
● **Discovering a fire**
● **Hearing the fire alarm**
● **Assembly points**
● **Calling the fire brigade**
● **Making power supplies safe**
● **Use of extinguishers**
● **Means of escape**
● **Evacuation of cats and staff**
If you discover a fire, call the fire brigade
Fire Drills: Fire drills should be conducted to simulate fire conditions ie, no advance warning given other than to

specify staff for the purposes of safety. The alarm should be raised on the instruction of management.

Do not call the fire brigade for a drill.

Do not evacuate cats for a drill.

CHAPTER 14

Principles into practice
Handling, grooming and tender, loving care

In a cattery there will be two sorts of handling of cats. First of all there is picking up, checking over, grooming or giving medication, which are necessary to the safety and wellbeing of the cat. Secondly, there is time spent interacting with and stroking the cats. Both types should be done with care, experience and confidence. If you have staff you should ensure they know how to pick up a cat properly and how to tend to the special handling needs of ill or disabled cats.

Handling cats in the boarding situation establishes a friendly bond between the cats and their carers, which can only be a good thing. However, the extent and type of handling should be judged for each particular cat and needs to be built up gradually. As we all know, under normal circumstances a cat will enjoy company and gentle handling. Be careful with new arrivals, it can take a day or two for them to become accustomed to you. Needless to say - some make it very clear that they do not want your affection!

Pushing too much attention onto a nervous cat can make it become even more withdrawn, so judge carefully what each cat needs and wants. However, most cats enjoy interacting with people, and owners want to feel sure that their cats are getting the type of caring attention that they would have at home. Most good cattery owners do have a genuine love for cats and enjoy the cats in their care - this will be obvious to the cats and their owners. If you can improve a cat's demeanour over its stay with special attention it's almost certain that the owner will be pleased. If you have time to spare - why not try some 'cat whispering' techniques.

Handling is also useful in picking up problems with cats such as an abscess or other lumps and bumps which may need immediate attention or can be mentioned to the owners on their return. All staff should be able to recognise common parasites or know when to alert someone if they feel the cat is not well.

Remember to wash and disinfect your hands between cats - handling is one of the most important ways in which diseases are spread. If you are grooming or cuddling a cat close to you, you will need to wear a disposable apron and replace it between cats. People visiting the cattery or dropping off their cats should not be allowed to touch the cats. Children should be warned that cats can scratch too.

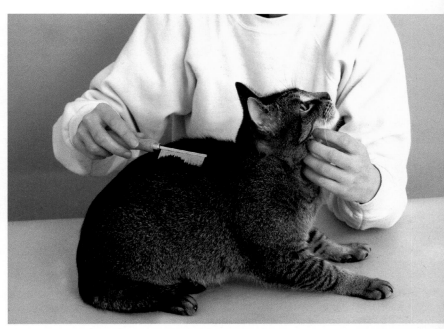

Grooming can be a pleasant and beneficial experience for cats. (Picture courtesy of Paddy Cutts, Animals Unlimited)

Grooming
Grooming can be a pleasant and beneficial experience for cats. If you do have long-haired cats in the cattery (Persians are still the most popular pedigree breed and there are many semi-long-haired pedigree and non-pedigree cats) then you will have to keep them looking good. Long-haired cats are particularly at risk of developing matted fur. Indeed some cats may come in with poor or matted coats and cattery proprietors often have to spend a lot of time sorting them out before they go home. Be confident in what you are doing and once the cat realises that nothing bad is going to happen it will get over its anxiety. Short-haired cats may also enjoy being groomed. Your basic grooming implements should be:

◆ A metal comb with teeth closer together at one end than the other
◆ A slicker brush
◆ A wide-toothed comb
◆ A smaller comb, similar to the above, intended for kittens and short haired cats

- ◆ A flea comb
- ◆ A good quality bristle brush
- ◆ A soft (preferably used) toothbrush
- ◆ Nail clippers, cotton wool, a large towel, and for any colour longhair cats other than black, Johnson's Baby Powder

Some cats prefer to be groomed on their owner's lap and will feel settled on yours (take a plastic chair into the run); double up the towel and place it over your knees, to protect your clothes and give the cat a sense of security. Talk to the cat all the time you are grooming; it is the tone of your voice rather than what you are saying which is important. The object of the exercise is to reassure the cat that you will not harm it, and that you are to be trusted. Most cats enjoy their one-to-one grooming sessions, especially those which were accustomed to it at a very early age. You may prefer to use a grooming table (some cats will prefer this to close handling) and cattery owners often use a small fold-up table which can be wiped clean and used in the cat's run. Depending on the size or accessibility, the shelf in the run can also be used. Some proprietors do the grooming as a two-person job, one holding and one grooming. It very much depends on the experience and confidence of the groomer and the temperament of the cat!

Be firm with the cat, without hurting it or causing any distress. As its trust in you grows it will gradually relax and enjoy the experience. By laying the cat on its side in your lap, talking to it gently, comb in one hand, and the other giving a gentle stroke or tickle, you will be in a position to gently restrain it should it become uneasy.

You can trim the fur on the bottom of the feet with round-ended scissors. Cats using litter trays often get pieces of grit trapped between their toes.

Using the toothbrush gently comb the face-fur under the chin - most cats love this - then progress to the top of the head and behind the ears. Hopefully, by the time you have done this for a few minutes the cat will be relaxed enough for you to take another comb and start combing the neck area. This is the place where early tangles tend to develop. If the cat becomes uneasy, stroke its head while still combing. Obviously, if at any time it becomes really distressed you must stop combing and go back to using the toothbrush on the face - some cats take longer than others to trust humans bearing combs!

The ideal way to groom a long-haired cat is from tail to head, but a cat which is unfamiliar to you will probably be reluctant to let you near his rear end unless it is fully relaxed and trusting. Be patient. The object of the exercise is to comb the fur from the roots to the tips and this cannot be done on a long coat by grooming downwards from head to tail as you will very easily glide the comb over small tangles which very soon become major knots. It is important NOT to try to turn the cat on its back, in order to groom its tummy, until it is confident that it will not be harmed. The 'belly-up' position is a very vulnerable one and many cats do not like it.

The main area where the knots develop are under the chin, behind the ears, under the armpits and in the groin area. By having the cat on its side it is possible to access these areas, by lifting one leg at a time, without completely exposing the under-belly. If you need to cut out knots, use round ended scissors and proceed with great care - get a pair such as those used by the vet to trim away knots which cannot be teased apart. Do not go overboard - some owners do not want to see a shorn cat on their return (even if you

have removed tats that have been there for a very long time). Try to do it as carefully as possible - however, it is time consuming.

Great care must be taken not to pull the fur or to apply the comb too rigorously, as the skin can be fragile and bruise or tear if this is done. If a tangle appears in one of these areas it is usually possible to place a couple of fingers between the skin and the tangle whilst combing it out. This relieves the pressure on the skin.

If at any time while you are combing its body the cat becomes uneasy, it is always a good idea to pick up your toothbrush. Give the head a few more strokes or tickle gently in a place where the cat enjoys being touched - usually under the chin, on top of the head or behind the ears.

As a general rule of thumb use your finest-toothed comb on the cat's head, progressing to the one with the widest possible teeth for its tail. If tangles develop in the under-arm area, comb through the worst of them with a wide tooth comb, then go through the fur with a smaller toothed comb ensuring that the coat is free flowing before you stop. The same applies to the groin area, which can become quite curly, especially in warm weather.

If you have a cat which gets particularly dirty around its bottom, you may need to wash it. If it is particularly bad it may be necessary to clip the fur away. However it is best to get the client's permission to do this - the owner of a show cat may not be impressed with a short back and sides at the tail end with a show coming up. If you see signs of fleas or worms while grooming and handling the cat, you will want to treat the cat. Check with its information card when it was last treated. Your veterinary authorisation form should have a section in which the owner gives permission for you to use a veterinary prescription-only medicine, such as Frontline or Advantage, on the cat to treat the fleas. (see page 106).

Cleaning ears
It is best not to poke anything into a cat's ear unless it is absolutely necessary. Cotton wool can be used to wipe away any greasy residue from just inside the ears. Sit the cat on your lap, facing away from you and gently turn back one ear flap; wipe it with cotton wool which, if the cat has really dirty ears, could be slightly moistened with warm water or even surgical spirit. Always squeeze the cotton wool out thoroughly so that there is no danger of liquid entering the ear canal. If you have to use surgical spirit, then use a dry piece of cotton wool to remove any residue. Do not use any ear preparations from any other cat.

If the cat has lots of very thick brown wax in its ears it may be a sign of ear mites (see page 107) and a vet should be consulted if the cat is in the cattery for more than a few days. If it is going home shortly mention this to the owner when the cat is picked up.

Wiping eyes
Cotton wool or a cotton bud is also used to clean the cat's eyes which in long-haired cats quite naturally exude brown liquid, especially after eating. This liquid, if allowed to remain on the face will cause an irritation which will prove quite difficult to cure, as well as leaving an unsightly stain on the face.

Dissolve 1 teaspoon of salt in 1 pint of warm water in a bowl. With the cat on your lap, dip a cotton wool ball into the salted water, wring it out and, wiping the corner of the eye down toward the mouth, very gently remove the brown liquid. You can use the thumb and forefinger of your left hand to gently draw the skin backwards until the skin in the corners of the eyes is 'tightened'. This will ensure that you can reach the very corner of the eye without harming the cat.

NEVER use the same piece of cotton wool for more than one wipe. A heavy build up of brown staining will take quite a few pieces to remove. When all the stain is gone wipe over the wet area with a dry piece of cotton wool. Needless to say, any sign of pus in the eye is a matter for the vet. Bathing is essential in the case of eye infections and the use of salt water is very beneficial. Again, never use a preparation from another cat to treat something which has not been seen or diagnosed by the vet.

Baby powder

Johnson's Baby Powder can be used in Persian or long-haired cats as an aid to grooming. It acts as a sort of dry shampoo which helps to keep the cat's coat tangle-free as it separates the hairs and makes them less likely to knot up. Initially, when you start shake a small amount of talc into one hand, rub it against the other and stroke the cat against the lie of the coat. Using both hands make sure that some of the powder goes down to the roots. Avoid the head at this stage but concentrate on the tummy, underarms and groin area. If you have used surgical spirit on his ears, you may find that now behind the ears looks a bit straggly. To combat this shake a small amount of talc onto a cotton wool ball and gently rub the area with this in one direction only. After you have applied the talc to the whole of the cat's body in this way, take your toothbrush to groom behind the ears and your bristle brush to remove every last trace of talc from the body. You should now find that every hair is separated and your long-haired cat will look fluffier and stay tangle-free for longer. At the end of grooming give your cat a treat, a piece of cheese or cat treat.

Bathing

Very occasionally a cat will come into the cattery and will need to be bathed. Most people have never attempted to bath a cat. It must be carried out in an escape proof room. Some catteries provide a grooming service and will have a specially equipped grooming room. Otherwise it may be best to use your own bathroom. If you are taking the cat out of its own pen make sure that you place it in a clean basket (preferably its own) for transportation to another part of the cattery - never carry a cat in your arms where it can escape. Make sure it does not come into contact with any other cats.

If you are washing the cat in your bathtub or sink, put a rubber mat in the bottom of the tub. The cat will have something to grip onto. Alternatively, use a plastic storage crate as a cat bath.

Bathing should be done once the cat has been combed. Giving a bath can cause the tangles to 'set' when dry and prove almost impossible to brush out. Using a good quality conditioner (which is rinsed out carefully) will help in removing tats.

You can fill the tub/sink with warm water or use the shower attachment to wet the cat. Make sure that the temperature is comfortable, not too hot or too cold. Place the cat into the water. He will probably make a dash for it but hold him firmly until he relaxes.

Apply a baby shampoo (never use any type of human

Top right: Make sure that the water temperature is comfortable for the cat and wet him all over. **Middle right:** Apply the shampoo and lather, avoiding the eyes, nose and ears. **Right:** Wrap the cat in a towel and keep warm until he is dry. (Pictures courtesy of Paddy Cutts, Animals Unlimited)

medicated shampoo), using the same technique as you do for your own hair, minding the cat's eyes and ears. Give the cat a rinse and repeat the process with another shampoo if necessary. Hold the cat by the scruff if you want to shampoo the belly etc. Rinse again with either a shower hose on the taps or a jug of water - some cats do not like the sound of the shower. Use a conditioner and rinse off well if you wish. Be careful to avoid getting any preparations in the cat's eyes.

Wrap him in a towel, it is important to keep him warm until he is completely dry. It is at this stage that he will probably start purring. You can use a hair drier on a low setting whilst working through the clean and fluffy fur with a small slicker brush. When brushing, hold the cat firmly and work in a line in a methodical fashion, do not criss-cross. Be especially gentle around the head.

If the cat will not tolerate a hair drier make sure that you towel him dry as much as possible and then use the slicker brush to brush the fur out. Before he is completely dry go over with the slicker brush again.

Matted coats

Unfortunately there are some owners who tend to let their long-haired cats, particularly Persians, get badly matted. If the coats are not groomed daily this will happen. If the cat is in that bad a state the kindest thing is for the vet to shave all the coat off while the cat is heavily sedated or anaesthetised. Alternatively, taking great care, it might be possible to cut out the knots with some round-ended scissors. However, this is not easy and it is unlikely that the cat will sit still for long enough. It is sometimes possible, with some knots, to just tease them out with the fingers. Another tip is to use a stitch unpick from a sewing kit which is blunt ended and can help to gently tease out the knots.

Clipping claws

Claws can become overgrown, especially in older cats. To clip the claw use a safe clipper (again, visit a professional or the vet and see what type they use) and ask them to teach you to use the claw cutters safely. Expose claws by applying gentle pressure to the paw-pad, and don't forget to clip the dew claws on the front paws. Always cut straight across and only clip the white part of the claw. The pinkish coloured part is the quick which contains nerves and blood vessels and must never be cut.

Hygiene

Grooming equipment must be kept separate from owners' equipment and other cattery utensils. Create a grooming kit for the cattery and store in a separate area. Never mix grooming equipment from the cattery kit with your house pet tools. Use grooming tools left with you by cats' owners wherever possible. Clean and disinfect the equipment before the owners collect the cat. Remember to disinfect hands, shoes and all grooming equipment after completing the task.

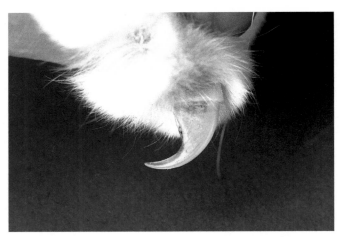

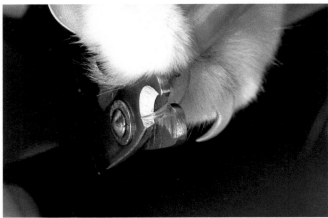

Above: Expose the claw by gently applying pressure to the paw-pad **Right:** Cut straight across the white tip of the claw. Avoid the pink-coloured quick

Part of the service?

Grooming can be very time consuming, especially if the cat comes in in bad condition. You may wish to put a fee on grooming in general for long-haired cats or just for cats which need more than the normal daily groom. As with all such matters you will need to make your policy clear to the owners at the outset.

CHAPTER 15

Staffing the cattery

Having the right cattery staff is vital. They will have hands-on care of the cats for some or all of the day and so will be responsible for ensuring they are comfortable, safe and happy. They also come into contact with the clients, therefore their approach and behaviour will be representative of the cattery — and you.

They must be trained in all aspects of disease control and understand why the disinfection and cleaning procedures are so important and should be carried out with great care. As important as this training is the understanding for the need for clear communication. Notification of potential problems to the cattery proprietor and all other staff members will substantially reduce work and worry.

Staff should at all times be clean and tidy. They should be aware of the potential they have to spread disease by their movements and through lack of attention to detail in cleaning, disinfecting and care of work stations and passages.

It is a good idea to involve staff in minor cat treatments if you feel they have the ability and enthusiasm to learn and participate, but it is essential that cattery proprietors pass on responsibility for medication and treatment of cats only to staff who are guaranteed to be able to carry out the treatments correctly. Failure to do so could easily lead to failure to medicate properly or to legal questions if a problem arises.

Hiring should never be done in a hurry. Make sure staffing needs are assessed with care. It may be that after a cattery has been running for a few months staff requirements decrease. Although it can take a few months, many experienced cattery proprietors are still surprised at the speed and efficiency that develop. Always ask for a reference from a previous employer or a personal testimonial from someone who has known the prospective employee for at least one year.

Advertising for staff
The cheapest, quickest and easiest way to get staff is through contacts, recommendation and other networking. Do not assume you have to advertise. Tried and tested methods include advertising in veterinary practices, local and church press and local colleges. Also, other local businesses and professionals may know who is seeking work and be able to advise on suitability. Do enlist the help of the nearest Jobcentre, they are interested in any kind of local vacancy and will do your recruiting free of charge. If placing advertisements make your notice attractive but short and to the point. Make hours, pay and essential experience required very clear in this first instance - it will save you a lot of time on the phone!

It is important at the time of advertising to have established your staff policy and considered the options for compromise. A well constructed contract agreed at interview will save explanation, disagreement and embarrassment later. A useful rule of thumb is that employing someone costs 1.17 to 1.2 times their wages (for National Insurance Contributions etc).

Suggested contract inclusions
An offer of employment has been made and accepted as follows:

(Employee's name) is employed as (job title) from (date). Cattery assistant to work at (location) for (hours - min and max).

Payment: To be weekly in cash. Additional earnings payable with following weeks wage. Payment will be made net of tax and national insurance contributions where applicable. It is understood that where wages are below contribution thresholds or are casual earnings, the employee takes responsibility for declaration of self-employment or notifies benefit agencies.

Notice: To be four weeks from Friday of week presented by either party.

Leave: 20 days holiday per year will be paid. These may be taken individually or together but must be agreed in advance where possible. Further unpaid absence will be at the discretion of the employer but will be fairly considered in cases of special events and circumstances. Sickness pay will be made at minimum hourly rate for up to 10 days per year.

Training: Employee will be thoroughly trained in all areas of cattery work, including some management.

Health and safety: Both parties agree to follow cattery policy on Health and Safety and to comply with statutory requirements at all times. This includes training in use of fire equipment and use of accident report book. Employer will provide a safe environment with toilet and first aid facilities and necessary protective clothing.

Demeanour: Employee agrees to represent cattery, in dress, behaviour, cleanliness and client relations in a conscientious manner.

Interview
Interview prospective staff as soon as possible. An enthusiasm

for your staff will rebound. Hold interviews in a comfortable and relaxed atmosphere after showing the applicant around your cattery and explaining what the post involves. In a good interview, the candidate should talk 75 per cent of the time while you listen 75 per cent of the time. For 25 per cent of the time you ask questions, tell about the job, etc. Have two copies of a contract to hand so that difficulties can be discussed. An obviously good person may well be worth a review of your requirements. Follow up any references immediately and remember that even an unsuccessful applicant should receive a letter of thanks. Remember to keep details of applicants who came a close second, just in case you need to find replacement staff in a hurry!

At interview take the applicant on a detailed tour of your establishment (this can be omitted if you feel the candidate is obviously unsuitable). Explain very fully the nature of the employment and all areas of responsibility. Explain all the training you can offer and the possible advantages of this. Present a copy of the proposed contract and discuss. Discuss family commitments and how they may affect both parties (school holidays etc). Ask for references. Take note of the applicant's overall manner. Do they speak confidently and clearly?

Will they be able to deal with telephone enquiries? Can they make sufficient eye contact? Do they answer questions fully, openly and with ease? Do they ask questions? Are they clean and tidy?

At the end of the interview ask the applicant if he or she has any questions and give them an opportunity to withdraw - they may have not known what to expect and be embarrassed about this or they may have reservations which you can address.

Ask where they saw or heard about the vacancy (free market research!).

Ask the applicant to take a copy of the proposed contract away with them for further consideration.

Explain that you will be in touch within one week by letter but would appreciate them informing you as soon as possible if they decide against the post.

Payment
Be careful to ensure you have taken advice regarding changes to employment laws (minimum wage, age and hours) since the publication of this manual.

Cattery staff are traditionally paid weekly in cash. It is unlikely that staff, who are almost always part time, will prefer alternative arrangements.

Pay staff promptly on an agreed day and privately by use of wage packet or envelope. A standard weekly amount can be paid with any extra due paid the following week. This will allow you to make up pay packets well in advance.

Tips on staff
Be as understanding as possible in matters of illness, family problems and lateness, etc, but be aware that these areas can create difficulties for the cattery and keep the employee mindful of this by keeping a time sheet on which anomalies are noted. There is no need for confrontation if an employee feels he can rely on his employer's understanding, but also knows his record can be monitored.

In a close working environment, such as a cattery it is more important than ever to establish and maintain a co-operative and amiable atmosphere. Regular small gestures of appreciation are the key to this. Staff need to be complimented and thanked where appropriate. They will be thrilled to see you have

noted and remembered birthdays. Take an interest in their lives outside of the cattery. Perhaps an annual cinema/theatre outing together could be arranged.

It is certain that a small bonus paid occasionally (after a particularly busy season or extra effort and help) will be appreciated.

Holiday cover
Try to establish dates for staff holidays as early in the year as possible and be as understanding as you can regarding family ties. If you have more than one member of staff you may find they work things out at least as well as you do and can be left to stagger time off. If you have week-end staff or young people in college for example, they will be invaluable during the summer months and possibly at Christmas time.

Health and safety
According to the Health and Safety at Work Act 1974, any organisation employing four or more people must have a written safety policy which deals with the health and safety of its staff. This policy statement must be signed and dated by the proprietor and revised and updated regularly. Put the document where all can see it.

It should include details of normal safety procedures and a risk assessment of possible hazards in everyday running, with relevant precautions and arrangements for dealing with emergencies such as injury or fire.

Information on Health and Safety at work is available from the local authority and from the Health and Safety Executive (HSE).

Staff must be familiar with the position of fire extinguishers and know how to use them. They should know the position of the main electricity switch.

Read and follow the instructions carefully on Health and Safety literature for products used in the cattery. No chemicals should ever be mixed.

The employer is responsible for the state of all equipment used and to provide safe working conditions. Employees have to carry out the job in a safe manner.

Wear rubber gloves and appropriate protective clothing, including wellington boots, as needed, eg, when handling chemicals like bleach, or when working with cats in isolation. Clothing for working with isolated cats must be kept separately.

Have adequate toilet and washing facilities should be available for the staff.

The Employers' Liability Act, 1969, requires employers to have valid insurance against liability for injury or disease sustained by their employees. Display the Certificate of Insurance.

Public Liability Insurance is also needed as it is the employer's duty to ensure the safety of themselves, staff and visitors.

Accidents and first aid
Record accidents and any 'near misses' in an 'accident book'.Report accidents to the proprietor. If someone is hurt or taken ill at the cattery, get help from someone competent. Serious accidents which may involve time off work must be reported as instructed in the regulations.

Report any damage or fault in electrical equipment or wiring to the proprietor immediately. It is required that all electrical fittings and equipment are maintained in a safe condition.

Staff should provide their own painkillers or other medicines. Keep at least one first aid kit. These are readily available eg, from St John Ambulance.

It is essential that everyone who works in the cattery has up-to-date inoculations against tetanus. If scratched or bitten, wash the affected part immediately and well. In the case of a bite, medical treatment should be sought as soon as possible as all bites should be treated with antibiotics.

Hazardous substances

Control of Substances Hazardous to Health (COSHH) Regulations 1988

These regulations deal with the handling of chemicals and other hazardous substances. They also deal with diseases transmitted from animals to people - zoonoses, eg, toxocariasis and toxoplasmosis. Advice on risks and precautions at work must be drawn to the attention of the staff (see below).

All insecticides and disinfectants should be used strictly in accordance with the manufacturer's instructions. Sheets are available from the manufacturers which explain the risks and the precautions to be taken by the user. These hazard sheets should be available to the staff who must be made aware what each substance is, what not to do with it and what to do if an accident occurs. Know what you keep in the cattery (keep a list/index) in the front of a ring binder with the materials' Safety Data sheets.

Zoonotic diseases

Zoonotic diseases are those transmissible from animals to man. Although these hazards are few, you need to take precautions and be aware that there can be problems. Fortunately, most feline zoonotic diseases are rare, although many myths regarding disease risks, and misinformation is often spread through ignorance or fear. In reality, many more people become sick each year from food-borne illnesses than ever fall ill from contact with cats.

Practising common sense together with a good hygiene routine, including careful handling of litter trays and routine treatment of cats with fleas and other parasites, significantly reduces the possibility of disease transmission from cats to humans.

Some important zoonotic diseases

◆ Cat bites and scratches

Most cats carry *Pasteurella multocida* in their mouths. Streptococci and fusiform species are often also present. Bites can result in deep implantation of any or all of these organisims so that severe infections commonly occur. Similarly deep scratches frequently become infected - it is strongly reocmmended that a doctor is seen and that this information is passed on. Tetanus status should be checked at the same time - anyone working in a cattery should ensure that their tetanus vaccinations are up-to-date.

◆ Fleas

Fleas are extremely common on cats and although the common cat flea cannot live on humans, they can bite humans and cause skin irritation. Fleas should be controlled by regular cleaning and spraying of the environment with a flea control preparation in addition to regular treatment of all cats for fleas.

◆ Ringworm

Ringworm (dermatophytosis) is one of the most common zoonotic diseases derived from cats. Cats should always be checked for suspicious lesions, and gloves worn if ringworm is suspected. Your veterinary surgeon can help in screening and identifying cats with suspected ringworm and treating any confirmed cases. It is important not to let children have direct contact with ringworm-infected cats, and careful hygiene precautions are necessary when handling such cats (wear disposable gloves and protective clothing). Attention must also be paid to environmental hygiene as ringworm spores are resistant and can be shed into the environment in high numbers. If any skin lesions occur, immediate medical advice should be sought.

◆ Toxoplasmosis

Toxoplasmosa is a parasite that infects cats and many other mammals, including humans. It is primarily a concern for pregnant women as, if infection occurs during pregnancy, damage can occur to the developing fetus. Most human infections come from poor meat hygiene, handling uncooked meat or eating undercooked meat. However, for a short period after they are first infected, cats may shed eggs (oocysts) in their faeces, and this is another potential source of infection for humans. Because of this, it is recommended that litter trays should always be emptied and disinfected on a daily basis (the eggs don't become infectious to humans until more than 24 hours after they are shed in the faeces), and that pregnant women are not involved in cleaning litter trays.

◆ Intestinal worms

Very rarely, humans can become infected with a cat roundworm (Toxocari cati) or the tapeworm (Dipylidium caninum). These infections are very uncommon (canine roundworm infections are more common in people), but regular worming of cats for both roundworms and tapeworms is an important part of the health care of all cats.

◆ Campylobacter and salmonella

These are two intestinal bacteria that can be a cause of severe gastrointestinal disturbances and can affect many animals, including humans. Infection in humans is usually through the food chain and infection from cats is rare, although they can be a potention source. Routine hygiene precautions (eg, washing hands after handling a cat) should always be followed and particular care should be paid to handling cats with diarrhoea. If the diarrhoea is prolonged, severe, or contains blood, veterinary attention should be sought to identify the underlying cause of the diarrhoea. If campylobacter or salmonella is identified, specific treatment and monitoring may be required.

◆ Cat scratch disease

Cat scratch disease (CSD) is a rare condition characterised by swollen lymph nodes and sometimes other signs (eg, fatigue, muscle pain, sore throat) that can occur following contact (eg, being bitten or scratched) with a cat. CSD is an uncommon disease and serious illness is very rare. The main organism responsible for this disease (Bartonella henselae) appears to be quite common in cats, but transmission to humans is very inefficient. Transmission of this organism between cats appears to occur mainly via fleas.

CHAPTER 16

Relationship with clients

While most people go into cattery work because they like cats, being able to deal with people is vital to the smooth and successful running of the cattery. Good communication will ensure that you have all the information you need about the cats in your care and a good relationship with your clients will mean they will use you again and again – vital to the success of your business. They will also recommend you to their friends and colleagues – the best form of advertising you can get.

Cattery clients really do cover every section of society. You will encounter characters of all types and temperaments. The key to successful relationships with your clients is to take your cue from their behaviour and behave accordingly. Attempt to 'read' the new customer and respond to their needs rather than your requirements. Take the time to listen to everything they want to tell you and to their stories about their cats (regardless of how common the story is). This interaction is where the bond between you is formed and the repeat business is won, beyond of course the proper care of their animal.

Maintain a smart appearance for you and your staff and ensure that any areas of the cattery that clients are likely to visit have been recently checked. Make sure you know the name and sex of their cat – this may take a little time and effort at the beginning but will make all the difference to your relationship.

Details of the information you require from your client can be found in the administration section of this manual.

Telephone contact

The secret of successful telephone business is to keep your objectives clearly in mind. A chatty cat owner on the telephone can lead to you having half the information you need at the end of the call. Establish the customer's requirements as soon as possible. Get as much information as possible as soon as possible. Become familiar with the cats name, breed, sex, etc, so that you can carry on your conversations with your client with confidence and in a reassuring manner. If a booking is unavailable, politely explain why you are so busy, suggest an alternative cattery, advise them to contact the FAB for other listed catteries and ask the customer to call next time. You may ask them for their name and address and say you will send information on the cattery for future use – you then have them on your database for future contact. The very fact that you were so helpful may give you a second chance with this client. Jot down information about cat the and

owner as you converse and write down details of bookings made over the telephone immediately. Tell the customer you will forward confirmation and cattery details to them. Remember to offer the customer directions to your cattery and to ask them for an estimated time of arrival.

Some owner types you may encounter
Elderly
Take great care with elderly clients, particularly those who are single or widowed - they have a particularly close relationship with their cats. Without patronage or condescension do as much as you can to help. Offer to carry the cat basket and other items to their car. Bear in mind that the elderly customer may have difficulty moving and may be hard of hearing. Many elderly people are lonely, so try to give enough time for a chat. A regular elderly customer who you know is not wealthy may appreciate a small discount.

Disabled
On realising that the client is disabled, think ahead and check your checking in/out procedures for difficulties they may encounter before they occur. Do as much as you can to alleviate difficulties but endeavour not to be seen to be doing so. Beyond the usual 'how are you?' discuss client's health only if the subject is raised by them. This is also where your planning ahead will also come into play – if you have built corridors wide enough to take wheelchairs then disabled visitors can actually see their cats into the cat unit and will appreciate being able to look over it for themselves.

First-time client
An owner bringing a cat for boarding for the first time may well be nervous. You need to be very friendly and professional and, without patronising, explain procedures in as reassuring a fashion as you can. Showing your affection and enthusiasm for your new boarder will put your new client at ease as their main concern will probably be the cat being unhappy without them and in a strange place.

Distressed
A client upset for whatever reason will usually tell you all about it. Be very reassuring over the cat's stay: this will help them to feel more positive. Take as much time with the client as they need: you have an opportunity to help. Be very careful when checking cat and booking information with this client.

Doting

The doting owner is often the talkative one. Don't be afraid, after an appropriate length of time, to indicate that you must get on with other things, but do not hurry them when they are settling in and saying farewell to the animal. This client may well bring a lot of items from the cat's home and may even bring it's food. They are not questioning your ability, but recreating the cat's home environment makes them feel easier about leaving it. Make sure this client feels able to telephone you while they are away for news of the cat.

Distant

A shy, distant or austere client is best treated in a quietly professional and calm friendly way. If their attitude is formal, respond in kind. Don't hurry through reception or departure but be succinct.

Awkward

Occasionally you will encounter a client who will simply seem a little dissatisfied with a lot of things. Bear in mind that the client chose to use your cattery and accepted the terms and costs in advance. Answer each quibble with an honest and straightforward response, remaining confident in your ability. You can be sorry that a customer has been dissatisfied but remember (and point out, if necessary) that the vast majority of your clients are not.

Note on children

Be watchful of clients who have their small children with them. Adorable or not, they are a risk to cattery security. Please ask the client, upon entering the cattery, to ensure that the child does not put fingers through wire, does not open doors and does not run about - keep one eye on the child/children - repeat request to parent if necessary - and cross your fingers!

Angry customers

When dealing with an angry customer remember that they are behaving in a particularly emotional fashion which is probably temporary. It is imperative that you remain calm, take their complaint seriously but not personally. The following guidelines may help:

- Remember that the complaint is a problem that you have, even if it is not your fault. The customer needs a grievance addressed and you are the best person to do this. Try to take control of the situation, whether you are at fault or not. Under no circumstances fight back.
- Listening is the key skill. Listen carefully to the customer's complaint. This will allow the customer, if they are uninterrupted, to let off some of the steam of the initial anger and allow you to understand and assess the problem.
- Explain that you understand why the customer is so upset. Reassure him or her that you wish to resolve the matter then decide calmly whether you think the complaint is justified.
- If the fault is yours accept responsibility, make no excuses and adopt a humble tone. If you need time to come up with a solution or response tell the customer and commit to getting back to them at a specific time - and do this. Assure the client that you intend to take responsibility for the fault and do so. Obviously the solution will depend on the specific problem.
- Keep in touch with the complainant and agree with them a suitable solution.

- If you are quite sure that you are not at fault explain in a calm and friendly way what you think has happened. Avoid laying blame directly on the complainant. Continue to use a tone indicating that whilst the problem is not your fault you wish to agree a solution. Explain in detail why you do not feel responsible and ask the complainant to get back to you after a little while to discuss what can be done. This will give you both time to reassess the situation.
- If the complainant becomes increasingly angry and is determined to hold you responsible when you genuinely are not, you must explain calmly that to become more heated is making the situation worse and explain that you'll have to terminate the conversation and continue to address the problem only in writing. If at this point you believe that the problem will escalate, and if you do receive a written compliant, it may then be time to seek legal advice. You will at least know that you have done your best to deal with your customer and care for your business.

Remember that you and your client have discussed all aspects of boarding with you, that you have explained all of your routines and procedures and that you have all the necessary consent forms completed by the owner. Your attention to detail will never prove more valuable than now.

Sickness or death of cat

In the event of a cat becoming ill whilst in your care it is essential that the owner understands that the situation has been fully explained to the designated contact person - and to the cat's own veterinary surgeon. Be prepared to give a full and detailed account of the illness and your response to it, and offer to take part in any necessary follow up treatment. Make sure that your client realises that you have paid extra attention to the cat and have real concern for it.

The death of a cat in your care is something we hope will never happen. Nevertheless, the possibility has to be accepted especially as many very old cats are now left in catteries on a regular basis. Make very sure the owner is aware of the event before the animals collection date. One of the kindest ways of dealing with the bereaved owner is to write (hand write if possible - it's much more personal) to the client, if possible so that the letter is waiting for them upon their return home. Express sympathy for the client and your own sadness, perhaps refer to remembering how sad you felt at the loss of a cat of your own. At the same time, very gently make it very clear that the contact and the cat's veterinary surgeon were aware of the situation at all times and that any disposal has been decided upon by them or have been carried out according to the client's wishes on the consent form. The client will need to know immediately where the cat is. Endeavour to take the cat to it's own veterinary surgeon for storage or disposal if the designated contact cannot give you specific instructions or this has not been ascertained beforehand. Understand that the bereaved client may need to visit or telephone you: be ready to offer comfort and support. If possible, a reduced or nullified invoice is suggested. (See also page 68).

Euthanasia

If the death of a cat in your care has been by euthanasia, follow the advice relating to death, but be sure to be able to tell your client that the decision was made and/or verified by the cat's own veterinary surgeon. Also be sure to give the designated contact advance warning of the procedure.

If at all possible, in all of these cases, speak to the cat's owner and contact. Many owners now have mobile phones or can leave hotel telephone numbers. Some owners who are not too far away may choose to come back to deal with these situations themselves and to say goodbye to the animal.

Abandoned cats

If a cat is not collected at the arranged time try telephoning the owner and the contacts. You will probably find the contact very helpful at this point. If you can get no help here and begin to feel that the cat has been abandoned it would be wise to contact the animal's vet. Many things can go wrong in life and it is always possible that an owner has no way of contacting anyone or addressing the cat's situation. Try to be patient and understanding. Keep in touch with the contact you have been given and the animal's vet. The cat obviously must be looked after and it falls to you to continue caring for it until a resolution is found. If it becomes clear that the poor cat has been left you should contact an association of cat protectors such as Cats Protection and ask for their help in temporary fostering and eventual re-homing. Perhaps you could seek a temporary home for the animal among people you know well and trust. Keep the contact and vet informed at all times. Write letters to the owner's address and employ any means you can think of (perhaps your local radio has a pet-watch slot). Do not lose touch with the cat as it may be difficult if an owner shows up a long while later.

Death of a cat's owner

Occasionally a cat's owner will die while the cat is boarded with you. In most cases relatives or friends will let you know and between them will find a home for the cat. You may have to be somewhat adaptable and may have to keep the cat longer than first organised, but if you have space this can be overcome. If you find out that the owner has died but nobody claims the cat you can be in a rather difficult situation.

The legal situation is thus – as cats are 'property' then they would theoretically follow other property in a deceased's estate. So the cat might be mentioned in a will. If not specifically mentioned, it would go to the legal 'next-of-kin'. If there are no next-of-kin, property goes to the state. From a practical perspective, a cattery owner should find out who is dealing with the deceased's estate, someone usually does. The fate of the cat should then be discussed and agreed.

CHAPTER 17

Health of boarded cats
Working with vets and assessing health

It is essential to build up a good relationship with a local veterinary practice. In this way the cattery knows that it will get a reliable service and prompt action if it needs it, and the practice knows that they will be used sensibly by the cattery. In most areas there are generally two or three veterinary surgeons' practices. Talk to them and find out if one specialises in small animals, with particular reference to cats. Invite the practice to visit the premises and discuss how your businesses can work most efficiently together, eg, whether you can see a vet outside normal clinic hours, whether you can take a cat to the surgery or the vet comes to you etc. If the practice has a chance to look around and are impressed with your business they may spread the word among their clients too, as they are often asked to suggest a good cattery.

Many minor problems that arise with cats in the boarding cattery may not need veterinary attention, but it is always better to seek veterinary advice too early rather than too late to establish whether immediate attention for an animal is required, or if supportive home care is possible. Provided that a clear description of the cat's general condition is given, the veterinary surgeon is generally able to assess whether or not the cat should be seen and to suggest any action or treatment that the boarding cattery proprietor can carry out. Whenever there is any doubt, you should always consult your veterinary surgeon for advice.

It is usually better to transport a very sick or injured cat to your veterinary surgery rather than call a vet out to the cattery because the equipment needed to investigate and treat the problem fully will only be available at the surgery. It is also important to telephone the practice prior to arriving with a very sick or severely injured cat, particularly out of normal working hours in case the surgery is locked and to allow time for the vet and staff to prepare for the emergency. All of these issues should be discussed with the practice so that everyone is aware of the arrangements between the two businesses.

This veterinary section is aimed at giving you some background knowledge of some of the conditions which may arise in the cats you are boarding and how best to deal with them. It aims to help you to decide whether veterinary assistance is required and, if so, how urgently. Situations such as severe respiratory distress, collapse, severe vomiting and bleeding are obvious emergencies and a cat showing any of these signs will need urgent veterinary attention.

The cat's condition and any treatment prescribed by the veterinary surgeon should be noted on its record card. Any treatment prescribed must be administered as directed by the veterinary surgeon until the full course has been given. Treatment should not be stopped early, even if the cat has completely recovered, and further veterinary advice should be sought in any cats that fail to improve or which deteriorate while receiving treatment. As discussed previously (see page 46), it is important to obtain consent for investigation and treatment of an ill cat in your care before the cat is admitted to the cattery.

Assessing health
Most cats arriving at a boarding cattery will be in good health and will remain in this state throughout their stay. In some cases, however, cats with pre-existing medical problems may be boarded, or health problems may develop while the cat is in the cattery.

At the time of admission to the cattery, it is important to obtain a brief medical history from the cat's owner, ascertain the cat's current health status (in particular whether it is receiving any veterinary treatment) and perform a visual and manual examination of the cat in its owner's presence.

The following information should be obtained from the cat's owner:
◆ The cat's age and sex, whether neutered or not
◆ The cat's normal diet and feeding regime
◆ Any particular preference for particular types of cat litter
◆ Preventive medicine:
  ● Vaccinations
  ● Flea treatment ⎤ what has been given and when
  ● Worm treatment ⎦ was this last done?
◆ Any known allergies or problems with veterinary drugs, eg, reacted badly when anaesthetised, allergic to antibiotics etc
◆ Previous medical problems – what were these, when did they occur, does the cat suffer from any long-term effects of these?
◆ The cat's current health status:
  ● Are the cat's appetite and thirst normal?
  ● Any diarrhoea, vomiting, coughing, sneezing, weight-loss, discharges from eyes/nose etc?
  ● Any problems with urination or defecation that the owner is aware of?
  ● Find out whether the cat has recently had any fights or accidents because problems such as abscesses can take some time to develop.

- Check whether the cat has been abroad recently (see chapter 20)
- Contact details for cat's normal veterinary surgeon

A lot of information can be gained from a visual examination and observation of the cat. Take the cat to its pen and examine it in the owner's presence. If there is a problem, be it fleas, a wound or a discharge from the nose or eyes, make a written record and ensure that the owner is aware of this. This will cover you should the owner return and swear that the cat did not have that problem when they left it. You can complete the admissions veterinary form (see example on page 47) and ask the owner to sign it. The form provides information on the cat's current condition and gives the proprietor permission to call for veterinary assistance should that be necessary during the stay. Some catteries send out the veterinary form when a booking is made so that the background information can be filled in before owners come in with the cat and thus save time on the day of admission.

Visual examination
Points to look for during the visual examination:
- What is the coat condition?
- What is the nutritional state of the cat, ie, is it emaciated, dehydrated etc?
- Is there a nasal, ocular or oral discharge?
- Are there any obvious injuries or abnormalities?
- Is the breathing normal, noisy, rapid, laboured, etc?
- How does the cat behave, ie, is it aggressive, stressed, relaxed etc?

Manual examination
If the cat is calm a brief manual examination can be performed. Below are the pointers for recognising a healthy cat – if you recognise a problem with any of these then they should be pointed out to the owner and noted on the form.
The following are pointers to a healthy cat:
- The healthy cat is bright and alert
- The eyes are clear and bright with no discharge
- The ears are clean with no dark brown or black waxy discharge
- The nose and face are clean with no sign of discharge
- The coat is glossy and parasite-free
- The skin is supple
- The cat is neither too thin nor too fat, with no muscle wastage
- There is no obvious stiffness or pain in joints and limbs
- The mouth and mucous membranes are pink
- There is no foul odour from the mouth
- There are no bad teeth or mouth ulcers

After a few days you may be able to ascertain that:
- Urine is passed apparently without discomfort – normal cats pass urine two to three times a day
- The appetite is good
- Faeces are firm and brown and passed without straining or discomfort. Normally cats pass faeces every 24 – 48 hours
- There is no presence of roundworm, tapeworm or blood in faeces.

Again, if you notice problems with any of these points then they should be noted on the cat's card and veterinary assistance sought if necessary.

The following are important pointers to the presence of underlying disease:
- There is apparent weight loss or the cat is very thin or lethargic
- The cat has no appetite
- There is an increase or decrease in frequency of defecation or urination
- There is diarrhoea
- There is straining or apparent pain on defecation or urination
- Faeces are fatty or greasy with an unusual smell
- There is fresh blood, 'changed' blood (black tarry faeces), mucus or slime in the faeces
- The cat is drinking excessively
- The cat is vomiting
- There is increased breathing effort or rate

NB Increased breathing effort may denote stress, eg associated with travel to the cattery or it can indicate serious illness or disease. Open-mouth breathing in cats is usually an indication of serious disease. Urgent veterinary advice should be sought if a cat has any breathing difficulties which do not settle very quickly.

A daily chart should be completed for each cat and include a record of eating, urination and defecation, any problems such as vomiting or diarrhoea or notes of unusual behaviour.

Boarding cats with medical problems
Provided an infectious condition does not exist, the fact that a cat is currently receiving medication is no reason why it should not be admitted to a cattery. However, the proprietor must ensure that whatever form of treatment is prescribed has been carried out. In this situation, it is especially important to obtain a thorough medical history before the owner leaves the cattery. It is also essential to have contact details for the cat's normal veterinary surgeon, so that if any further problems arise, they can be consulted for advice.

Some of the more common current problems that cats are admitted with are discussed in detail in chapter19 and include diseases like hyperthyroidism and chronic renal failure.

Vaccination
All cats admitted to the cattery should be vaccinated for cat 'flu (feline herpesvirus and feline calicivirus) and feline enteritis (feline panleukopenia virus). Additional vaccines such as for feline chlamydiosis (now referred to as *Chlamydophila felis*) or feline leukaemia virus are not required for disease control in a cattery situation because cats do not come into direct contact with each other. Vaccines should be current (up to date) with the final vaccine of the primary course or the booster vaccine for subsequent vaccinations, given at least seven days before admitting the cat. If the cat is admitted sooner than this, there is a danger that its immunity may not be fully boosted, putting it at risk of succumbing to diseases upon infection.

The course of vaccination must have been completed as follows:

- **Cats with no previous vaccination history**
  Both sets of injections to have been completed at least 7 – 10 days before entry to the cattery.
- **Annual booster**
  Not more than 3 months overdue. If over 3 months, a single injection to maintain protection, administered at least 7 – 10 days before entry to the cattery.

A veterinary vaccination record must be seen

Homoeopathic vaccines

Vaccines work by stimulating an immune response to specific structural proteins (antigens) associated with a particular disease-causing infectious agent. This immune response provides protection against development of disease when the cat is subsequently exposed to the infectious agent. A crucial aspect of vaccination is the presence of antigen in a form that is recognised and responded to by the immune system. As homoeopathic vaccines do not contain any of the infectious agent or its associated antigens, there is no rational basis for their use. Furthermore, use of homoeopathic vaccines is potentially dangerous because most diseases vaccinated for are very serious and homoeopathically 'vaccinated' cats cannot be assumed to be protected against these. Admitting such 'vaccinated' cats to a boarding cattery is particularly hazardous since any environment where many cats are housed together carries a higher risk of spread of infectious disease and the stress associated with boarding may lower the cats' resistance to development of disease, increasing their vulnerability.

When to worry about cats in your care

In many cases, it will be obvious when you need to worry about a cat in your care and seek veterinary advice. In some cases, this may be less obvious and the following advice may be helpful:

Is the appetite normal ?
Veterinary advice should be sought if :
◆ A cat hasn't eaten for more than two days, sooner if the cat has any known medical problems or appears unwell
◆ If the appetite is very excessive, especially if the cat is losing weight. This is not usually an urgent problem so you may decide to wait for the owners to return and discuss the problem with them
◆ Pain or difficulty in eating is seen
◆ The cat's appetite is generally poor, especially if it appears unwell in other ways, eg, depressed, vomiting etc.

Is the cat passing urine normally ?
Veterinary advice should be sought if :
◆ Small amounts of urine are being passed very frequently and especially if pain or straining are seen
◆ Bloody urine or urine containing blood clots is seen
◆ The amount of urine produced increases dramatically during the cat's stay
◆ The appearance of the urine is abnormal, eg orange colour, cloudy appearance
◆ Pain or difficulty noted when urinating
◆ No urine is passed for twelve hours or more and especially if the cat is noted straining to urinate. This is **an emergency** as urinary obstruction is potentially fatal
If any of these are seen, it may help your vet if you can collect a sample of urine (where possible) for them to examine (see page 96 for information on how to do this)

Is the cat passing faeces normally ?
Veterinary advice should be sought if :
◆ No faeces are passed for three days or more
◆ Pain or difficulty passing faeces is noted on several occasions
◆ Large amounts of fresh blood present in the faeces on one occasion, or small amounts present on several occasions

◆ 'Changed blood' (digested blood) is suspected. In this situation the faeces may appear black and tarry
◆ The cat has diarrhoea which does not resolve following 24 hours starvation, followed by introduction of a bland diet such as white fish or chicken and rice
◆ The cat has diarrhoea of any duration and appears unwell in itself
If the faeces appear abnormal in any of these ways, it may help your vet if you can collect a sample for them to examine.

Is the cat's thirst normal ?
Veterinary advice should be sought if :
◆ A marked thirst is noted, especially if water consumption over a 24 hour period exceeds 100 ml per kg bodyweight. If the cat is otherwise well, this may not be an urgent problem so you may decide to wait for the owners to return and discuss the problem with them
◆ A cat fed dry food only is not drinking any water. Normal (24 hours) water consumption is between 40 and 70 ml per kg bodyweight, depending on the cat's diet.
Investigation of causes of an increased thirst usually includes examination of a urine specimen so if veterinary advice is sought, it may be helpful to collect a sample for the vet to examine. (see page 96 for information on how to do this)

Is the cat showing any other signs of illness ?
Veterinary advice should be sought if any of the following are present :
◆ Vomiting
  - which does not resolve following twenty-four hours starvation followed by introduction of a bland diet such as white fish or chicken and rice
  - any cat which is unwell in itself, especially if it is unable to keep fluids down
  - if blood or digested blood ("coffee grounds" appearance) are seen in the vomit
◆ Coughing
◆ Sneezing
◆ Discharges from the eyes/nose etc
◆ The cat appears depressed or listless, especially if other signs of illness are present
◆ Breathing difficulties, where:
  - The cat is breathing through the mouth, or
  - Laboured breathing is seen, or
  - The cat is breathless – taking more breaths per minute
◆ The cat has a seizure (convulsion)– see page 94 for more information
◆ The mucous membranes (gums, lining of third eyelid and eyelids), nose or skin appear an unusual colour, eg, jaundice (yellow) or cyanosis (blue). Cyanosis is an emergency situation.
◆ Sudden loss of vision (may be associated with high blood pressure and requires urgent treatment)
◆ Collapse – fainting or complete loss of consciousness as well as severe depression and inability or loss of desire to get up
◆ Paralysis of one or more legs

If at all in doubt, call a veterinary surgery for advice

CHAPTER 18

Storing and administering medicines

Legislation governing use of veterinary medicines

Several laws govern the handling, storage, prescription and use of veterinary medicines in cats. A veterinary medicine is defined as 'any medicinal product intended for animals and applies to veterinary medicinal products for sale in the form of proprietary medicinal products and ready-made veterinary medicinal products'.

Veterinary medicines are classified as follows:

1 **GSL – General Sales List**
   Any preparation falling into this category can be sold by anyone over the counter in any appropriate shop, eg, worm treatments available at pet shops. Many of these products are also available at veterinary practices and you do not need to be a client to purchase these for your animal.

2 **P – Pharmacy only**
   This category includes pharmacy prepared medicines which can be supplied over the counter by a pharmacist, or by a veterinary surgeon for an animal under their care. In practice, very few veterinary medications fall into this category.

3 **PML – Pharmacy and Merchants List**
   This category includes medicines supplied by a veterinary surgeon for animals under their care or by a pharmacist over the counter. Some worm treatments are included in this category.

4 **POM – Prescription Only Medicines**
   POMS are medicines that can be supplied by a veterinary surgeon for an animal in their care. They may also be supplied by a pharmacist, but only on a veterinary surgeon's prescription. This category includes many veterinary treatments such as antibiotics, vaccines and some flea treatments.

5 **CD – Controlled Drugs**
   Drugs in this group are also POMs but require even more strict control for storage and prescription, as these include drugs that may be abused, eg, morphine, some barbiturates.

Storage of drugs/the medicines cupboard

Medicines should all be clearly labelled with the animal's name and instructions for medicating – this should be done by the prescribing veterinary surgeon.

Drugs should only be given to the animal for which they were obtained and prescribed, unless directed otherwise by the prescribing veterinary surgeon. The complete course of treatment should be given and not stopped earlier, even if the cat appears to be cured.

Drugs should be stored according to the manufacturer's instructions in a place which is not accessible to the public or children. In most cases, a cupboard (preferably lockable) is acceptable although some drugs, such as insulin, need to be stored in a refrigerator. Storage areas should be well ventilated and clean. Food or drink should not be consumed in this area. Unused medication should not be kept by the cattery but returned to the prescribing veterinary surgeon for disposal.

Cattery owners should not store or administer any drugs unless these have been prescribed for that cat, by a veterinary surgeon. This includes use of flea and worm treatments. It is important to ask owners what worm or flea treatment has been administered to their cat when it is admitted (see consent form page 47) so that if either are noted when the cat is boarding, a veterinary surgeon will be able to prescribe appropriate treatment without any danger of drug overdose.

Storage and use of environmental flea sprays obtained from a veterinary surgeon is entirely appropriate as long as these are used according to the manufacturer's instructions. It may also be helpful to store the following in the medicines cupboard:

◆ Glucose powder or syrup
◆ Flea comb
◆ Cotton wool
◆ Pair of curved surgical scissors
◆ Grooming equipment (see chapter 14)
◆ Disposable gloves and containers for collection of urine or faeces (obtained from a veterinary surgeon)
◆ Tweezers

Medicating cats

You should always seek veterinary advice before giving a cat any medication. Medications that are available for cats come in a variety of different forms. Anything given to a cat (other than food) should be considered as a medication, including herbal remedies and tonics. It is important to remember that just because something is herbal it is not necessarily safe to give to cats. Treatment that is safe for other animals or humans may also have dangerous side effects in cats. Although it is possible to purchase a number of remedies from pet shops or chemists, it is strongly advised that all medication is obtained through a veterinary surgeon who will advise on the suitability of various drugs and who will be able to prescribe far more effective products than are available over the counter. Many medications can have side effects and may prove fatal if used in the wrong combination, so it is essential that your vet is informed if an animal is already being treated with any preparation.

Unless you are very experienced in handling cats, medication is most easily given if there are two people available. Sometimes, holding a cat firmly by the scruff will be enough to control it – but don't be tempted to try this with an aggressive cat unless you want to end up nursing a very painful bite! Alternatively, you can try wrapping the cat up in a large towel. Spread the towel out and place the cat in the middle; then wrap the towel firmly round the cat, ensuring that its front paws are kept inside. If necessary, kneel down with the cat between your knees to stop it struggling. Some cats can be very difficult or even impossible to medicate so, if you are having problems, contact your veterinary practice for advice, as the medication may be available in other forms that are easier to administer.

Giving tablets, capsules or liquids

Some of these can be given mixed with food; tablets can be crushed or capsules opened and their contents sprinkled on the food. However, some cats will refuse to eat food that has been tampered with in this way! Medication is better given in a small quantity of strongly flavoured food prior to the main meal. Sometimes mixing the medication with a little butter and making it into butter balls, can be successful. Some tablets/capsules are not suitable for crushing/opening so this should always be checked with a veterinary surgeon first. If the tablet is sugar coated, then cutting it into smaller pieces or crushing it, may make it very bitter and unpalatable. Another option to those already mentioned, is to buy empty gelatin capsules from a chemist into which the cat's treatment can be put. These can then be used to dose the cat in the same way as described for giving pills and capsules (see

later). If a cat is receiving several drugs at the same time then these can all be put into the same empty gelatin capsule. Some treatments must be handled with care and disposable gloves must be worn if this is the case – your vet will tell you if this is necessary (eg, some chemotherapy treatments).

Your veterinary surgeon will show you the most effective position to hold the cat for administering tablets and it is usually easier to aim the pill accurately if the cat is put up on a table and held firmly. The mouth is opened by holding the angle of the jaw with the thumb and forefinger of one hand, tilting the head backwards, while using the forefinger of the other hand to depress the lower jaw (see below). The pill or capsule should be placed as far back in the cat's mouth as possible and pushed over the back of the tongue with a finger inserted into the mouth or using a syringe and a small amount of water. Then, holding the mouth shut, with the

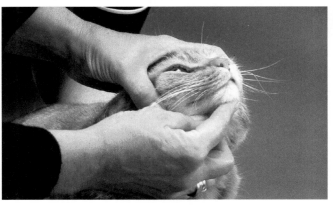

Top: Giving a pill. Hold the cat's head as shown, tilt it backwards and using the forefinger of the other hand, depress the lower jaw.
Middle: Place the pill as far back into the mouth as possible.
Above: Hold the head in a normal position and stroke the cat firmly on the throat until it has swallowed the pill. Sometimes it is helpful to syringe 2 to 5 ml of water into the cat's mouth to encourage swallowing (see p 89 for advice on how to give liquids).

head in a normal position, stroke the cat firmly on the throat until it has swallowed the pill. If the cat keeps spitting the tablet out, it is usually better to have a break and try again a few minutes later, otherwise you will both become increasingly stressed as the pill becomes more and more sticky, ending up everywhere other than where it is aimed! Pill poppers can also be used to dose cats with tablets or capsules. The pill is put into the pill popper which is then put into the cat's mouth to dispense the pill at the back of the mouth without any risk of being bitten. The cat should be offered food or water afterwards as recent research has shown that a pill can sit in the throat for several hours and may cause inflammation.

Liquids by mouth should be given gently and aimed at the roof of the mouth to minimise the risk of the cat breathing in the mixture, which can cause pneumonia. The easiest way to administer liquids is to use a syringe, inserting the nozzle in the gap behind the canine teeth. The liquid must be given slowly to avoid choking.

Above: Giving liquids by mouth. Liquids should be given gently and slowly, aiming at the roof of the mouth to minimise the risk of the cat breathing in the mixture. Insert the nozzle of the syringe in the gap behind the canine teeth.

Using eye drops and eye ointment
The cat should be held firmly and the head tilted upwards and the eyelids gently parted with the thumb and finger of one hand. A few drops or a line of ointment can then be placed on the surface of the eye or along the lower lid. Close the eyelids and massage gently to spread the medication over the whole of the eye surface.

Inserting ear-drops
The cat should be held firmly and the head tilted so that the ear to be medicated is uppermost; the required number of drops should then be placed into the ear canal and the

Above: Giving eye drops or ointment. To give eye ointment hold the cat's head tilted upwards and part the eyelids gently with the thumb and finger of one hand. Place a few drops or a line of ointment on the surface of the eye or along the lower lid. Close the eyelids and massage gently to spread the medication over the whole of the eye surface.

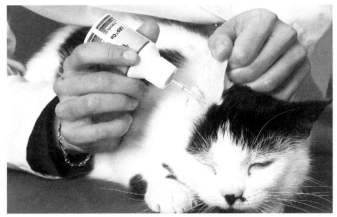

Above: Inserting ear drops. Hold the cat firmly and tilt the head so that the ear to be medicated is uppermost.

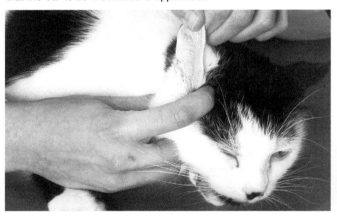

Above: Squeeze the required number of drops into the ear. Hold on to the ear flap to prevent the cat shaking its head. Massage the ear base gently.

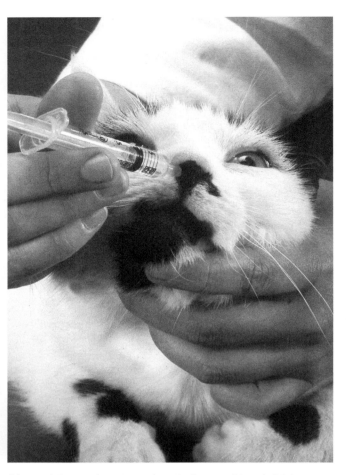

Above: Intranasal treatment is not often used to administer medicines

dropper bottle removed while still squeezed. Hold on to the ear flap with one hand to stop the cat shaking its head. The ear base should then be gently massaged and, if the drops have been administered correctly, a 'squelchy' noise is heard. Any wax or debris on the ear flap can be gently removed using cotton wool.

Do not use cotton buds as these may become detached in the ear canal and never poke around inside the ear canal.

Applying a spot-on preparation

Left: Part the hair down to the skin at the back of the neck **Right:** Apply the product onto the skin. Some preparations recommend that the product is applied at two different locations on the back of the neck, with half the tube dispensed at each.

Administering a subcutaneous injection

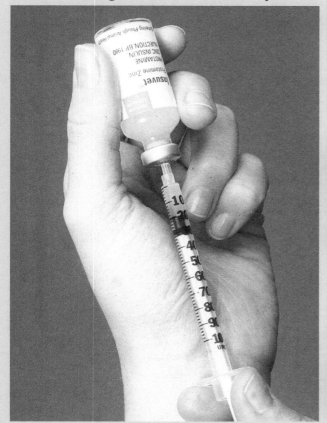

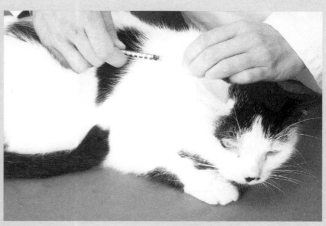

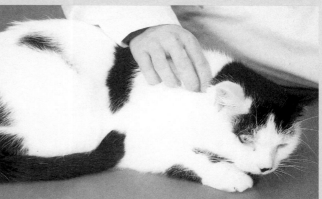

In diabetic cats, (see later section on this disease) it may be necessary to give daily or twice daily injections of insulin under the skin (subcutaneously). Occasionally, other diseases will require medication given by this route.

The injection technique should be taught by a qualified veterinary surgeon or veterinary nurse. Injection techniques can be taught using saline (salt solution), learning how to withdraw the required amount into a syringe and then how to safely inject this into a patient. Subcutaneous injections are given in areas where the skin is loose, usually the scruff of the neck. The plunger should always be pulled back prior to injecting the drug to check that the needle is not in a small blood vessel. This would make the injection intravenous - which is potentially very dangerous, especially in the case of drugs like insulin.

Injections should always be given using a new sterile syringe and needle which should be safely disposed of. Following single use, needles should be placed in the needle guard, and syringes and needles stored in a safe place such as a locked medicines cupboard before returning to a veterinary surgeon for appropriate disposal.

Above left: Draw up the required amount of drug into a sterile syringe using a sterile needle. In the case of insulin, the drug should be removed from storage in the refrigerator and gently mixed (by rolling the container between the fingers) before withdrawing any insulin for injection. This is important to ensure adequate mixing of the insulin suspension. See also page 95. (preferably have an assistant to gently restrain the cat)
Top: Lift a fold of skin over the scruff (back of the neck). Insert the needle through the skin and pull the plunger back slightly. If blood appears in the needle/syringe then the injection should not be continued. The needle should be withdrawn and the procedure repeated from the beginning. If no blood appears, it is safe to continue and administer the injection. **Above:** The needle is withdrawn.The site is gently massaged to distribute the drug in the area of injection.

CHAPTER 19

Health of boarded cats
A – Z of common health problems

FAB has an extensive list of information sheets on feline diseases and behaviour problems which is constantly being updated and added to. The conditions covered below are the most common problems which a proprietor may encounter and are approached from the boarding point of view. FAB can be contacted for additional information. A * denotes that there is an FAB information sheet available on this subject.

Abscesses

Cats may come in with an abscess or develop one soon after admission. An abscess is an accumulation of pus under the skin caused by infection, usually through a bite or other wound. It is usually seen as a painful swelling or, after it has burst, as a wound discharging pus. Common sites are around the head, neck and at the base of the tail. If the abscess has burst, clean the wound with a saline solution (add one teaspoon of salt to a pint of warm water to make this) trying to express the pus by pressing gently around the wound. An abscess that has not burst may need to be lanced and drained by a veterinary surgeon. Consult your vet for additional treatment (eg antibiotics) or immediately if the cat seems to be in pain, or is otherwise unwell (eg not eating, depressed and quiet).

Amputation
- see Disabled cats

Anaemia

Anaemic cats have fewer red blood cells than normal. The red blood cells carry oxygen to tissues so affected cats are usually depressed and lethargic. If the anaemia occurs gradually (for example in cats with chronic renal failure) then the affected cat usually adapts its lifestyle to cope with this, not showing signs of disease until the anaemia is very advanced. If anaemia develops rapidly, for example following blood loss, the affected cat is likely to be very weak and collapsed and needs urgent assessment and treatment from a veterinary surgeon.

Severely anaemic cats may have obviously pale mucous membranes (gums, membranes of the eyes) and a pale nose if this is unpigmented.

Important causes of anaemia in cats include feline leukaemia virus (FeLV), feline immunodeficiency virus (FIV), feline infectious anaemia (FIA), and chronic renal failure.

Arthritis

Inflammation of the joints causing pain, stiffness, difficulty or reluctance to move can be seen following previous trauma to the joint (eg, road traffic accident), as a result of generalised joint disease (eg, immune-mediated polyarthritis) or as a degenerative disease affecting elderly cats. Arthritic cats may be admitted to a cattery with painkiller therapy. Most painkillers used are NSAIDS (non steroidal anti-inflammatory drugs) which have potential side effects including vomiting which may contain blood. If vomiting is seen, treatment should be withdrawn and the cat's veterinary surgeon consulted for advice.

A cattery proprietor may need to ensure that cats have help getting onto shelves (or lower the shelf) or, in penthouse style catteries, supply graded gentle steps to the sleeping accommodation. A stiff cat flap may also pose problems and can be left propped open wide if necessary.

Ataxia
- see Incoordination

Ataxia is the term for a wobbly, drunken or incoordinated gait.

Bladder disease *
- see Lower urinary tract disease

Bleeding
- see Haemorrhage

Blindness

Cats may develop blindness if they suffer from severe hypertension (high blood pressure), severe trauma, glaucoma or other ocular conditions. It is important to keep everything (eg food bowls, litter tray) in the same place each day so that the cat is able to learn where these are, and not become confused or distressed.

Blind cats should be approached quietly and gently while speaking to reassure the cat of your presence.

Penthouses may not be suitable for blind cats which may have difficulty with the ramp and finding their way to the sleeping accommodation.

Breathing problems

Laboured breathing or difficulty in breathing is known as dyspnoea

Right: Cat showing breathing problems. Unlike dogs, cats seldom breath open-mouthed – if there is no obvious cause (such as car travel which may have been stressful) urgent veterinary advice should be sought.

and is characterised by an increase in breathing effort or rate and sometimes breathing through the mouth. Dyspnoea can be short-lived following a stressful episode, such as a car journey to the cattery, and should rapidly settle down to normal. However, it can also be associated with severe disease and urgent veterinary advice should be sought concerning any cat with breathing difficulties.

Bruises

Because most cats have a thick hair-coat, bruises are not generally seen and can often be difficult to feel. The hair-coat is also protective, so bruises tend to be less common in cats than in people. The most common sign that a cat may be bruised is pain in a localised area. This may be apparent when that area is gently felt or if the cat resents being stroked over a particular part of its body which it normally enjoys or tolerates. In the majority of cases, minor bruising does not require treatment and will resolve over a 24 to 48 hour period. More severe bruising, where there is moderate to severe pain when the area is touched, requires veterinary advice, as there may be other deeper injuries which need to be specifically treated. Any sign of pain should always be dealt with as a matter of urgency.

Calicivirus *
- see Respiratory disease

Cancer

Cancer is the lay term for malignant neoplasia. Neoplasia is persistent, purposeless, proliferation of cells. Malignant cancers are so-called because as well as growing at their starting location, they invade adjacent tissues and spread to other near and distant sites of the body.

Treatment of cancer may include surgical removal, radiotherapy (use of radiation exposure to kill cancer cells) or chemotherapy (use of drugs orally or by injection to kill cancer cells). (See Lumps and bumps, Lymphoma).

Cardiomyopathy *

This is the medical term for disease of the heart muscle. Thickening (hypertrophy) of the heart muscle is most common in cats (see Heart disease).

Cat flu
- see Respiratory disease

Cheyletiella
- see Parasites (mites)

Chlamydia *
- see Feline chlamydophilosis

Chronic renal failure
- see Kidney disease

Chronic rhinitis *

Also referred to as 'chronic snuffles' – this is one of the potential long term consequences of cat flu. Affected cats usually suffer from a nasal discharge and sneezing associated with bacterial infection of nasal tissues which have been damaged by previous flu virus infection. Although the snuffles usually resolve completely when the cat is given antibiotics, many affected cats will relapse as soon as this treatment is stopped. Most cats with chronic rhinitis are otherwise bright and well and have a normal appetite.

Collapsed or unconscious cats

A veterinary surgeon should be contacted immediately if a cat collapses or loses consciousness. If unconscious, the cat should be placed on a bed, kept warm and if breathing difficulties are suspected, it may be worth checking the mouth for any sign of obstruction. The cat should be taken to a veterinary practice as soon as possible for emergency treatment.

Conjunctivitis

Inflammation of the membranes lining the eyelids and third eyelids is called conjunctivitis. There are many potential causes of this but important causes would include flu virus infection and chlamydophilosis. Affected cats often have a sore eye which they hold closed, discharge from the affected eye/s and red or swollen conjunctival membranes may be visible. Any cat developing signs of conjunctivitis whilst at the cattery should receive veterinary attention as soon as possible.

Constipation *

Constipation is prolonged retention of faeces and may manifest as infrequent, absent or incomplete defecation. There may be no obvious clinical signs, though chronically constipated cats can become dull and depressed, may be seen vomiting or showing signs of discomfort and you may notice the cat straining in the litter tray. Some constipated cats will pass small amounts of liquid (which may contain blood) around their impacted faeces and this can be mistaken for diarrhoea by an inexperienced carer. Many normal cats will only pass faeces once every one or two days, particularly if they are being fed a highly digestible, low residue diet. Some long-haired cats will go through periods of constipation when moulting. Regular grooming to remove loose hairs and to prevent build-up of a hair-ball in the stomach or intestine is helpful. Veterinary advice should be sought if the cat is seen straining to pass faeces, if the cat shows signs of pain when defecating or if no faeces are passed for three days or more. Veterinary examination is necessary to confirm the diagnosis of constipation and to determine its cause and appropriate treatment. Many cats will respond to medication and dietary changes but laxatives or enemas should never be used without veterinary supervision.

Convulsions

The veterinary term for a fit is a seizure or convulsion. Affected cats may behave strangely before they have a fit, although most often seizures occur when the cat is asleep. During the seizure, the cat may foam at the mouth (excess salivation), lose consciousness, have rigidity or tremors of the muscles, or paddling movements of the limbs. Incontinence (faecal or urinary) may also be seen. In most cases, the seizure itself lasts for less than two minutes. A cat may be weak and disorientated for some time after having a fit.

If a cat is seen having a seizure, it should not be handled unless it is in danger of hurting itself where it is fitting (for example, if the cat is on a shelf it could fall off, it should be gently placed on a bed on the floor). Any stimulus such as touch, light and sound can prolong the fit so the cat should be quietly observed while it is fitting and lights, radios, etc, should be turned off. The observer should time the length of the seizure and seek urgent veterinary advice if the fit does not stop after two minutes. If the cat recovers from one seizure only to have another or a series of fits soon after, urgent veterinary advice should again be sought. In all cases, it is helpful for the observer to take notes describing the seizure and how long it lasted, as this will aid veterinary assessment and diagnosis. A veterinary surgeon should be contacted in all cases where seizuring is seen.

If a diabetic cat is seen seizuring, there is a risk that this is due to low blood sugar levels (hypoglycaemia). Before seizuring, affected cats will usually show other signs of low blood sugar levels such as disorientation, weakness/wobbliness, searching for food and behaviour changes such as licking their lips. If seen, rapid treatment is required as the seizures resulting can be fatal. If the cat is still conscious and will eat, it should be fed. If this is not possible, glucose powder or syrup (honey or sugar would be second choices) should be put onto the cat's gums. A notable improvement should be seen with five minutes. Veterinary advice should be sought immediately as severe cases may need to be hospitalised for intravenous glucose administration and further stabilisation. See also epilepsy

Coronavirus *
- see Feline infectious peritonitis

Coughing
Coughing can be a sign of bronchitis (inflammation of the major airways), pneumonia or asthma. Rarely, coughing can be associated with respiratory infections such as cat flu or bacterial infections such as Bordetella bronchiseptica. If a cat develops a cough while in the cattery, veterinary advice should be sought.

Cowpox
- see Poxvirus

Cuts and minor wounds
Cats with minor injuries may be admitted to the cattery or these may result from squabbles with other cats if several cats from the same household are kept as a group. As in humans, minor cuts often require little attention and will heal quickly. Cuts may not be immediately obvious, particularly in dark coloured cats where blood is less easily noticeable. You should suspect that a cat has been cut if there is a localised area of hair that is stuck together, if the cat is showing signs of an injury such as lameness, or if it resents being stroked over a particular area.

Most cats will manage minor wounds themselves. You can help by gently bathing the area with warm salt water (saline solution) and cotton wool. To make a saline solution, add one teaspoon of table salt to one pint of warm water. Cuts are best cleaned by using a relatively large amount of water or saline solution to flush out any dirt or bacteria rather than rubbing or dabbing at the wound. The application of cream after cleaning is unnecessary and most cats will only lick the cream off unless the area is covered.

It is important to differentiate small cuts from penetration injuries such as cat bites which produce a deep wound even though the opening is small. Penetrating wounds will need veterinary attention. Larger cuts with a gaping wound edge, profuse bleeding or injuries where there is damage to structures such as the muscle layers beneath the skin, will need urgent attention. Also, if there is marked lameness or sensitive organs such as the eyes are involved, a vet should see the cat straight away because recent clean wounds can be repaired much more successfully than older wounds. At home, the wound can be gently washed out with a saline solution and covered with a non-stick dressing as advised by your vet.

If wounds are left untreated and become infected, flies may lay their eggs causing serious problems when these hatch into maggots which invade the infected tissue. This type of problem is common when a cat has a wound that has gone unnoticed for a period of time. Urgent veterinary attention is required if this problem is seen.

Deafness
Cats may develop deafness if they suffer from inner ear problems or have had to have major ear surgery. Some elderly cats will also become quite deaf. Deaf cats should be approached gently making your presence known to the cat by approaching it from where it can see you coming.

Dehydration
Dehydration can develop in any cat that is losing more fluids than it is taking in, for example in vomiting/diarrhoea, very depressed cats that have stopped drinking and in cats with chronic renal failure. Subtle dehydration can be difficult to diagnose without a blood test but more severely affected cats may have sunken eyes (the third eyelids may become more prominent), dry or tacky gums and skin tenting. To assess skin tenting, a flap of skin, such as that over the scruff, is pinched and then lifted up and let go. In normal cats, the skin leaps back to its previous state almost instantly. In dehydrated cats, the skin tent stays for a few moments before gently creeping back to its normal position. If the dehydration is extreme, the skin tent will remain.

If a cat is thought to be dehydrated, veterinary attention should be sought as a matter of urgency.

Dental disease
- see Mouth problems

Dermatophytosis
– see Ringworm

Diabetes mellitus *
Occasionally, an owner may request boarding for their diabetic cat. Adequate care of a stable diabetic cat is possible in the boarding cattery, as long as the proprietor feels able to administer the necessary treatment and monitor the cat for signs of any problems, as outlined below.

Diabetes mellitus is a relatively common disease in cats, tending to affect middle to old-age neutered cats and it is more common in males than females. It is caused by a relative or absolute deficiency of the hormone insulin.

The insulin deficiency may arise as a direct failure of the pancreas to produce insulin, so-called insulin-dependant diabetes mellitus (IDDM) but in cats it is often the case that there is adequate production of insulin, but that the body's cells are unable to recognise or respond to this insulin, a condition known as non-insulin-dependant diabetes mellitus (NIDDM). There are a number of reasons why this might occur; obesity is a common cause of reduced sensitivity to the effects of insulin, some drugs (eg corticosteroids and progestagens) antagonise the effects of insulin and some natural hormones also have an anti-insulin effect, so that cats with Cushing's disease (excess production of natural corticosteroids) and acromegaly (excess production of growth hormone) also tend to develop NIDDM.

Clinical signs
The insulin deficiency results in an increase in blood glucose levels and the four 'classical' clinical signs of diabetes that result from this are weight loss, an increase in appetite, an increase in the volume of urine that is produced and an

increase in the amount of water that is drunk, to compensate for the increased urine production.

Diagnosis

Diabetes mellitus is suspected whenever the appropriate clinical signs occur but further tests are needed to confirm the diagnosis. Blood tests will show a persistent elevation in blood glucose levels (hyperglycaemia) in a cat with diabetes, however other conditions, and in particular stress, may also cause a transient rise in glucose levels so this can be a misleading finding. A more reliable blood test involves measuring the level of fructosamine in the blood, as this will only be elevated if the blood glucose has been high for most of the previous two to three weeks, as is the case in untreated diabetic cats.

When there is persistent hyperglycaemia there will also be 'overflow' of glucose into the urine, so urine analysis can also be helpful.

Treatment

Diabetes mellitus is usually a treatable condition. Although long-term treatment does require commitment, it can be very rewarding to successfully manage this condition. Initial steps in treating a diabetic cat may involve removal of any of the predisposing causes for the diabetes eg appropriate dieting for an obese cat or withdrawal of drugs that antagonise the effects of insulin.

If there are no predisposing causes, or if their correction does not lead to resolution of the diabetes, specific treatment is required.

A small proportion of cats with NIDDM will respond to treatment with 'oral hypoglycaemic agents' - tablets that increase the amount of insulin produced and increase its effectiveness. These tablets are not suitable for all cats with diabetes but in some cases they can be useful.

However most cats will require insulin supplementation in the form of injections to control the diabetes. There are a number of different types of insulin available and different cats will respond better to one type than to another. Each cat is different in the way it responds to insulin and how much insulin it requires. It is therefore necessary to monitor the response to treatment very closely at first until a pattern has been established and it is common for a cat to be hospitalised at a veterinary surgery during this initial period. Once the cat has been stabilised (which usually takes a week or so), treatment can be continued at home. For most cats, this involves a single daily injection of a small dose of insulin. Very small needles are available for this, which cause no pain to the cat, and within a short period of time the procedure becomes very routine. Normally the insulin will be administered in the morning (usually between 7.00 and 9.00) along with 1/4 to 1/3 of the daily food, with the remainder of the food being given around eight hours later, when the insulin is at its most effective. Some cats will rapidly metabolise insulin that is given by injection and in those cases it may be necessary to use twice daily injections, spaced at 12 hour intervals, and adjust the feeding pattern accordingly.

Because of this individual variation in the response to insulin you must follow closely any advice given to you by the cat's veterinary surgeon.

Insulin is quite an unstable drug; it must be kept refrigerated or its effect will be less potent than expected. It can even be damaged by shaking the bottle - so careful handling is essential. Insulin suspensions are most frequently used. Before use, the suspension needs to be gently mixed by rolling the bottle or gently inverting it. Cats usually require a very low dose of

insulin at each injection, diluting the 'standard' insulin solution can be helpful to ensure accurate dosing, but this must be done by a vet and the diluted solution will then only remain active for about one month. See page 00 for advice on giving subcutaneous injections.

Diet and feeding regimes

The cat should be fed its usual diet according to the regime suggested by the cat's veterinary surgeon. Any changes to the type or amount of food, or meal times, can affect stabilisation of the cat's diabetes. The cat's insulin dose will have been established based on a particular feeding regime. Altering that regime will alter the insulin requirements and there is a risk that by changing the diet the amount of insulin that has been given will be inappropriate.

Monitoring the diabetic cat

It is important to monitor the following while the cat is boarded, and keep detailed records.

◆ Water intake (measured in ml for a twenty four hour period)
◆ Time insulin given
◆ Amount of insulin given
◆ Amount of food eaten and times fed

If possible it is helpful to monitor the cat's bodyweight. In addition, monitoring the amount of glucose and ketones in the urine (using urine passed in the night or first thing in the morning) may be suggested by the cat's veterinary surgeon. To collect urine, it is usually easiest to replace the normal cat litter at the end of the day with clean (washed) aquarium gravel or Mikki litter which is non absorbent cat litter available from a vet. Since neither of these will absorb urine produced overnight, a sample can be collected for testing by your veterinary surgeon, or they may supply you with a kit to test it yourself. If there is any marked change in the amount of glucose in the urine, this may indicate the need to alter the insulin dose, but you should never change the dose of insulin without first discussing it with the cat's veterinary surgeon. Changes in the insulin dose are usually based on trends in urine glucose concentrations as there is normally some day-to-day variation. In most cases, the dose of insulin is chosen on the basis of blood glucose measurements which are a more accurate indicator of response to treatment.

Insulin overdose

If a cat receives too much insulin, it is possible for the blood sugar level to drop dangerously low. For this reason it is important to be very careful in ensuring that the cat receives the correct dose of insulin. Careful mixing of the insulin suspension is an important part of this as if the suspension is not adequately mixed it may be possible to accidentally over or under-dose the cat.

The typical signs displayed by a cat with a very low blood sugar level (hypoglycaemia) are severe weakness and lethargy, shaking, odd behaviour (eg, aimless wandering, licking lips, miaowing), unsteadiness and even convulsions. If a diabetic cat shows any of these signs it is important to seek urgent veterinary attention. If the cat displays mild signs of hypoglycaemia then it should be offered food and encouraged to eat. If the more severe signs are displayed (collapse, and/or convulsions) a tablespoon of a glucose powder or syrup should be given by mouth immediately. As this is an emergency, it is useful to have a small amount of a glucose solution stored in a refrigerator for any cat receiving insulin. If no glucose is available, sugar or honey can be used instead. A noticeable effect should be seen in 5 minutes. A veterinary surgeon should be contacted immediately as the cat may need glucose by injection or, at the very least, some changes to its insulin regime.

When to be concerned about a diabetic cat in your care
Veterinary advice should be sought urgently if:
◆ Any signs of low blood sugar levels, or especially convulsions,are seen.
◆ If the cat is still conscious (eg walking with an unsteady gait or behaving strangely) it should be offered food which may help to increase blood sugar levels and avert more serious effects of low blood sugar such as seizures.
◆ If the cat is unconscious or will not eat, glucose powder or syrup should be put on the cat's gums. A notable improvement should be seen within five minutes (see also above section on insulin overdose and earlier section on convulsions).
◆ The cat appears unwell showing signs such as vomiting, diarrhoea, loss of appetite, depression, panting, dehydration or collapse. These may indicate ketoacidosis, an uncommon but life-threatening complication of diabetes.
Both low blood sugar levels and ketoacidosis can be rapidly fatal and immediate treatment is required.

On a less urgent basis, veterinary advice should also be sought if:
◆ The cat's demeanour changes. Most diabetic cats are very bright and well and any change in this can indicate poor control of the diabetes. This may be seen for a variety of reasons including mild/early hypoglycaemia or ketoacidosis, or if other complications such as urinary tract infection or pancreatitis develop.
◆ The cat's water intake increases significantly or varies hugely from day to day, as this may suggest poor control. Normal cats and well stabilised diabetic cats drink up to 70 ml per kg bodyweight every twenty four hours, depending on the diet fed (cats fed a tinned diet drink less than those fed a dry diet).
◆ The cat's appetite is very variable or is poor. This too can suggest poor control of the diabetes, ketoacidosis or presence of other concurrent diseases which are complicating control.
◆ If urine samples are being monitored for glucose and ketones and either –
   Increased or varying amounts of glucose are present in the morning urine sample or
   Any ketones are found at all (the vet should be notified of this immediately even if the cat appears well, as ketoacidosis can be rapidly fatal).

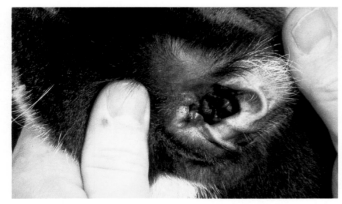

A quick look in a cat's ear is simple to do. It may show up obvious problems which need veterinary attention.

Diarrhoea *
Diarrhoea is not a disease in itself but is a sign that can reflect many different problems. Stress, change of diet and environment may all cause diarrhoea in an otherwise healthy cat. Diarrhoea can also be caused by diseases of systems other than the intestinal tract. When emptying or changing litter trays, it is important to check the faecal contents to ensure that diarrhoea is detected at an early stage. As with vomiting, if the diarrhoea is short-lived or is occasional, there is unlikely to be cause for concern. Starvation for 24 hours followed by a light diet of chicken or fish for a few days will be sufficient for most short-lived episodes. Veterinary advice should be sought if the diarrhoea is persistent, bloody, is very dark and tarry in appearance (suggesting the presence of digested blood) or is associated with other signs of ill health such as vomiting and weight loss.

If veterinary attention is sought, it may be useful to supply your vet with a faecal sample which should be stored in a fridge until it is submitted to them, ideally within 24 hours.

Disabled cats
It is sometimes necessary to remove a cat's leg for medical reasons such as cancer or severe fractures. Some cats have neurological problems which make getting around somewhat more difficult than normal and proprietors may have to adapt the cat accommodation to suit. Most cats cope with amputation well and soon adapt to getting around on three legs. There is no reason not to board an amputee cat. If you have a penthouse style cattery you may need to provide gentle small steps up to the sleeping accommodation if the ramp is rather steep. Likewise, all catteries may need to provide help up onto shelves. Also make sure the cat has no problem with the cat flap.

Ear infections *
Head shaking, ear twitching and holding the head to one side are signs of infestation or infection. The most frequent cause is ear mites (Otodectes). If the presence of a foreign body is suspected, there are any signs of loss of hearing or of loss of balance, a veterinary surgeon should be consulted for advice.

Eosinophilic granuloma complex *
This is a skin disease which most commonly causes red, raised swellings on the lips, skin or in the mouth. When present on the lips, these are often called 'rodent ulcers'. Eosinophilic granulomas can develop in cats suffering from allergic skin disease such as flea allergy and may respond to treatment for this allergy. If an eosinophilic granuloma is suspected in a boarding cattery, it is advisable to contact a veterinary surgeon for advice.

Epilepsy
Epilepsy is the medical term for a seizure or convulsion. Primary epilepsy (epilepsy without any underlying cause) can be seen occasionally as a cause of seizures in young cats. Epilepsy can develop as a secondary problem in cats that have suffered a blow to the head or in cats with brain tumours for example. See also convulsions.

Eye problems
There are many different types of eye problems which include, ulceration of the eye, foreign bodies (such as another cat's claw!) and cancer. Affected cats may show one or more of the following signs:
◆ Pain – holding the eye shut

- ◆ Swelling of the eye or eyelids
- ◆ Visible foreign body
- ◆ Change to the size or shape of the pupil
- ◆ Change to the colour of the eye surface or contents eg, clouding of the surface, bleeding into the eye

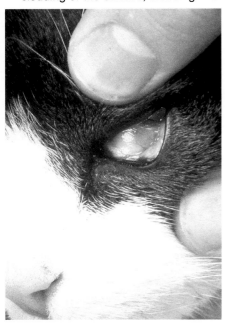

The cat's third eyelid is not usually seen - it is a thick membrane which can cover all of the eye. A small part of it may be visible in the corner of the eye closest to the nose.

Occasionally the cat's third eyelid (see above) may cover some part of the eye. This may be a sign that there is an eye problem or that the cat is somewhat unwell, for example in dehydrated or very thin cats the third eyelid may be visible. Often the cause is never ascertained and the eyelid goes back to its normal position where it cannot be seen.

If any of these signs are seen or if a cat suddenly appears blind, veterinary advice should be sought as a matter of urgency.

Feline chlamydophilosis * (formerly feline chlamydiosis)
Feline chlamidophilosis is caused by infection with a specialised bacteria called *Chlamydophila felis*. This name has recently been changed from feline *Chlamydia psittaci*. It is an unusual bacterium because it lives inside the cells of the body whereas most bacteria live outside the cells. For this reason, it does not survive well outside the body. The organism primarily infects the lining around the eye (conjunctiva) causing a persistent conjunctivitis (inflammation of the conjunctiva). It is most commonly seen in young kittens at around 5 to 12 weeks of age. It is not however, a cause of 'sticky eyes' seen in very

Cat suffering from feline chlamydophila (formerly known as chlamydia)

young kittens at 10 to 14 days of age. The incubation period of 4 to 10 days is followed by the development of a profuse watery discharge, with affected cats holding the eye closed or blinking more frequently (blepharospasm, blepharitis) and marked reddening and swelling of the conjunctiva result. Initially one eye may be affected but after 5 to 12 days, both eyes will usually become infected. After a few days, the watery discharge becomes thicker and may be reddish-pink in appearance with the conjunctiva appearing less swollen and more reddened. Most cats remain bright, though some will be off their food for the first few days and have a mild temperature. A nasal discharge and sneezing are occasionally seen. The conjunctivitis may persist for six weeks or more if left untreated.

As cats can continue to excrete chlamydophila for many months after recovery, during which time other cats can become infected, it is important that all the cats in the household are treated. Treatment should be given for at least four weeks and continued for a minimum of two weeks after signs of disease are no longer evident. It is common for 'flare-ups' of clinical signs to occur especially if treatment is stopped early. Protection against re-infection is poor and recurrent episodes of disease can occur, especially in a large group of cats where the disease can go round and round.

Treatment
As it is a bacterial infection, chlamydophilosis will respond to treatment with a number of antibacterial agents. Tetracyclines such as doxycycline, which can be given once daily, are the agents of choice. Medication is best given by mouth as it is difficult to apply ointment frequently enough to be effective. As stated earlier, treatment is required for four to six weeks in order to ensure elimination of the infection, and all of the cats in the household should be treated even if some of these appear to be healthy.

Control
Control is aimed at preventing close contact between infected and susceptible cats and should not be a problem in the boarding cattery situation. A vaccine is available that can be used in vulnerable groups, however its use decreases the signs rather than completely preventing chlamydophilosis.

Feline immunodeficiency virus (FIV) *
Feline immunodeficiency virus is a slow virus (lentivirus). Lentivirinae are characterised by very long incubation periods and slow onset of disease. Like HIV in humans, FIV is associated with a slow destruction of the immune system which eventually makes the cat vulnerable to other infections which would not normally cause a problem in a healthy individual.

Source and spread of infection
FIV is present in most bodily secretions, as well as the bloodstream. Transmission is thought to occur during fighting and biting, with FIV infection being particularly prevalent in male, free roaming cats, especially those with a history of fighting. Vertical transmission from the queen to her kittens is also possible - typically one third to one half of kittens born to an infected queen will be infected in this way.

Clinical disease
The clinical findings in FIV infected cats are very variable with few reliable diagnostic signs. Many cats have a history of recurrent bouts of illness, with non-specific signs such as lethargy, swollen lymph nodes, fever and weight loss. Most cats

will develop one or more of the following problems: gingivitis (inflammation of the gums), stomatitis (inflammation of the mouth), rhinitis (discharge from the nose), conjunctivitis, anaemia, skin problems or diarrhoea.

Diagnosis

FIV is usually diagnosed by demonstrating the presence of antibodies to the virus in the bloodstream since these are associated with lifelong infection with this virus. Most tests can be performed rapidly at a veterinary surgery, giving an on-the-spot diagnosis. However, research has shown that a significant minority (possibly up to 20%) of cats infected with FIV do not develop antibodies detectable on these tests, so these cats will appear as false negative results, ie, the test will give a negative result but the cat is actually infected with FIV.

Alternative tests are available at commercial laboratories and can be used if a false negative result is suspected. These include different antibody tests, and more recently, a test for viral genetic material (PCR test).

Kittens born to an FIV-infected queen acquire antibodies to the virus via suckling. This means that if their blood is tested for antibodies to FIV a positive result will be obtained, even though typically only around one third of the litter will be infected with the virus. These so called 'maternally derived antibodies' persist in the kittens' bloodstream until they are about 12 weeks old. In those kittens that are infected with the virus, it can take a further two months before they produce antibodies to the virus. This means that antibody tests should not be used to test kittens for FIV infection until they are six months old.

Treatment

There is no specific treatment for FIV currently licensed for use in cats although some cats respond well to human treatments such as AZT and Interferon. Essential fatty acids (such as oil of evening primrose) have been shown to have some beneficial effects, especially in cats in the early stages of disease. Reducing the exposure of FIV infected cats to other diseases is also important. This includes not feeding raw meat and discouraging the cat from hunting due to the increased risk of disease following toxoplasma infection, to which FIV-infected cats are more vulnerable. Restricting an FIV-infected cat's contact with other cats also helps to reduce the risk of acquiring infections such as cat flu and chlamydophila. Prompt and aggressive treatment of secondary infections is very important as an FIV-positive cat may not be able to mount the required immune response. Additional supportive treatments including intravenous fluids and blood transfusions may also be needed. In some cases, eg severe gingivitis, corticosteroid therapy may be beneficial. FIV-positive cats should be treated for worms and fleas regularly and vaccinated against flu and enteritis, if possible, using a dead vaccine. In the long-term, it is felt that virtually all FIV-infected cats will eventually succumb to disease and die although this is usually after many years of good quality life.

Control

FIV can best be controlled by reducing the spread of infection from fighting and biting. Aggressive FIV-positive cats must always be housed separately although other positive cats may be kept with uninfected cats if there is no fighting, as the risk of transmission of infection via social contact (grooming, sharing food bowls etc) is extremely low. Neutering to prevent vertical spread from queens to kittens and fighting between males should be undertaken as a priority. It is usually suggested that FIV-infected cats are kept indoors, at least at night, since this is when most cat fights occur. In addition, as stated under 'Treatment' this helps to limit the FIV-infected cat's contact with other infectious diseases to which it is more vulnerable.

Boarding FIV-infected cats

The major source of FIV is virus shed in the saliva of an infected cat. Unlike FeLV, non-aggressive close contact between cats (such as mutual grooming) is not efficient at transmitting infection and the main route of transmission is via a bite from an infected cat.

FIV-infected cats admitted to the boarding cattery should only be housed with cats from the same household and should not be allowed any contact with other boarding cats. This is a normal requirement for all cats in a boarding cattery in order to minimise the risk of transmission of all infectious diseases, so should not pose any problems to the cattery owner. Between handling cats from different households, the hands should be washed and there should be no sharing of food bowls etc between different pens.

FIV-infected cats may remain clinically well for several years and during this time require no special treatment. In the latter stages of illness, immunosuppression (deterioration in the body's immune function which can lead to an inability to fight infections) may result in recurrent infections and weight loss, requiring more specific treatment, and eventually euthanasia. Boarding of FIV-infected cats may therefore involve feeding a special diet and administration of medicines. Prompt treatment of infections is particularly important in FIV-infected cats so if a previously healthy FIV-infected cat becomes ill whilst boarding, urgent veterinary advice should be sought. If in doubt consult a veterinary surgeon.

FIV-infected cats may be admitted with ongoing medical therapy such as antibiotics or evening primrose oil (see section on medicating cats for more information). It is useful to have a complete history including contact information for the cat's own vet, should any problems arise when the cat is boarding.

Feline infectious anaemia * (FIA)

Feline infectious anaemia is caused by a small organism (most commonly known as Haemobartonella felis) which infects the red blood cells. This infection can, in some cases, lead to destruction of the red blood cells which causes anaemia.

Cats are very good at coping with anaemia until it is quite severe so it can be difficult to identify cats with this infection. Clinical signs include lethargy, poor appetite and depression. In severe cases jaundice (yellow discolouration of the skin and membranes of the eyes and mouth) can be seen and the cat may have a high temperature.

FIA is diagnosed by examination of a blood smear under the microscope or by using a probe to detect the organism's genetic material (PCR test). Infection does not always cause disease so treatment may only be required in cats with anaemia also present.

Anaemic cats with FIA may need a blood transfusion in addition to treatment with antibiotics (usually tetracyclines) and high doses of glucocorticoids to reduce the destruction of red blood cells by the cat's immune system. Often treatment does not completely eliminate the infection so recurrence of anaemia may occur at a later date. Cats with other diseases which suppress their immune function (such as FeLV or FIV) may be more prone to this disease and to having recurrent problems.

FIA is thought to be spread by blood sucking insects such as fleas although the exact routes of transmission of infection are not known. It is possible that cat bites, blood transfusions and other routes such as from a queen to her kittens may also occur.

If an FIA-infected cat is brought for boarding there should be no risk of transmitting infection to other cats in the cattery as long as normal precautions are maintained. The cat may be currently receiving medication when admitted and this should be continued, according to the prescribing veterinary surgeon's instructions. The veterinary surgeon should be contacted if any deterioration in the cat's condition is seen.

Flea treatment should be administered regularly, according to a veterinary surgeon's advice, in these cats in order to reduce the risk of spread of infection. If any signs of illness are seen in a cat that has been reported to have previously had FIA, veterinary advice should be sought as a matter of urgency in case further treatment is needed. It is possible that the stress associated with boarding may precipitate recrudescence (flare up) of a previous infection.

Feline infectious enteritis * (FIE)

Feline infectious enteritis is also known as feline parvovirus (FPV) and feline panleukopenia (pan = all, leuko = white, penia = lack of). A very effective vaccine for FIE has been available for many years now and so the main cases of death and disease are in unvaccinated cats and particularly kittens. Only vaccinated cats should be admitted to the boarding cattery for this reason. Because rescue cats are often unvaccinated, the mixing of rescue and boarding cats is not recommended as it can put boarded cats at risk if the virus is present. Strict hygiene precautions would need to be undertaken.

FIE was the first disease of cats to be shown to be caused by a virus. Parvoviruses are very dangerous as they are able to survive for long periods, sometimes even years, in the environment. Cats infected with FIE can continue to excrete the virus for at least six weeks following infection. Parvoviruses are resistant to many disinfectants and it is vital that an effective disinfectant is used.

Source and spread of infection

Feline infectious enteritis is spread by direct faecal-oral contact and also indirectly following contamination of the environment or objects by an infected animal, eg on food dishes, grooming equipment, bedding, floors, clothing or hands. Transplacental spread through the uterus to the unborn kittens can occur. Infection in late pregnancy leads to the under-development of the cerebellum an area of the brain concerned with coordination of movements. This is called cerebellar hypoplasia. Affected kittens often appear normal at birth but as they become more active, they show incoordinated movement, walking with their legs wide apart, a high stepping gait and tremors affecting the head and limbs may be seen.

These kittens usually adapt to cope with their disability and require no special treatment when boarded.

Clinical disease

In kittens over three or four weeks of age and adults, the virus causes severe enteritis, following an incubation period of five to nine days. If the immune response is not adequate to protect the cat, the virus will enter the bloodstream and travel to the bone marrow and lymph glands, leading to a marked decrease in numbers of white blood cells (leukopenia). The virus also infects the intestines where it destroys the rapidly dividing cells of the lining of the gut. Infected cats and kittens usually have a fever, are obviously depressed and will not eat. This phase is rapidly followed by severe vomiting and bloody diarrhoea. Occasionally kittens will be found dead, having shown no signs of the disease previously.

Treatment

No specific treatment is available and it is vital that any suspected cases are nursed in isolation as this is a highly contagious disease. Protective clothing must be worn and hands washed thoroughly after handling any cat or kitten suspected of having the disease. Where possible, one or two people who do not handle any other cats should be assigned as nurses. Cats often die from dehydration and massive secondary infection, so fluids and broad spectrum antibiotics are crucial. Severely dehydrated cats will usually require intravenous fluids and veterinary support is essential. Anti-emetics (to stop vomiting) can also be helpful. Good nursing care is vital to help sick cats and especially young kittens to recover from the disease.

Control

Feline infectious enteritis is far better prevented than treated. Highly effective vaccines are available and all cats and kittens should be vaccinated at least seven (preferably more) days before admission to the cattery in order to ensure that they are protected from disease (see page 84).

Feline infectious peritonitis * (FIP)

Feline infectious peritonitis is one of the major infectious diseases in cats. Although it is not a common disease, it is of particular concern since once the clinical signs of disease have developed, it is invariably fatal.

Source and spread of infection

Feline infectious peritonitis (FIP) is a coronavirus. Cats are commonly infected with enteric coronaviruses and these usually cause no or very mild disease such as diarrhoea. Cats may become infected with FIP virus or this can arise when an otherwise harmless enteric coronavirus mutates within an individual cat, generating new strains of the virus. These mutant varieties are most likely to cause disease in cats with very poor immunity. Young kittens, old cats and those with immunosuppressive diseases are most at risk of succumbing to disease following infection with FIP. Stress, caused by overcrowding, is also an important factor and will increase the risk of the cat developing concurrent infections. Weak kittens living in overcrowded conditions are more likely to develop FIP than strong adults living in small, stable groups. Whether or not a cat develops FIP will depend, not

Cat suffering from the wet form of feline infectious peritonitis (FIP) where the abdomen is distended with fluid

only on the strain of the virus to which it is exposed but also on the strength of its own immune system. It is thought that some cats are genetically more susceptible.

A major source of the spread of the virus is through infected faeces. Cats can also be infected by sharing food bowls or by ingesting the virus during mutual grooming. Cats kept in overcrowded conditions are most likely to receive a very high dose of virus, both directly by cat-to-cat transmission of the virus and indirectly from litter trays and the environment. Spread of the virus can be exacerbated by the difficulty of effective cleaning when there are a lot of cats housed together.

Clinical disease
FIP causes a wide range of different clinical signs. Most commonly, an infected cat will develop an accumulation of fluid in the abdomen, causing abdominal distension, or fluid will accumulate in the chest, causing difficulty in breathing.Where fluid accumulation occurs in the chest or abdomen this is known as wet or effusive FIP. In other cases, the signs may be more obscure referred to as dry or non-effusive FIP. Some cats will have a prolonged period of vague illness along with a fluctuating high temperature.

Diagnosis
Veterinary attention is essential to diagnose FIP but this diagnosis is sometimes very difficult. A number of changes can be found on routine blood tests that suggest FIP but these are not specific to FIP. Similarly, tests can confirm exposure to feline coronaviruses but exposure to these viruses is common in healthy cats as well as being present in those that develop FIP. Although some clinical signs and laboratory tests may be very suggestive of FIP, confirmation of a diagnosis requires a biopsy of diseased tissue or a post-mortem examination.

Control
Cats appearing healthy when admitted may develop FIP in the cattery due to precipitation of the disease by stress. Other cats from the same household may be at risk of developing the disease, particularly if they are very young, very old or immunosuppressed (for example FeLV or FIV infected), although in most cases FIP causes sporadic disease rather than an outbreak.

Admitting cats with positive coronavirus titres
As already said, blood tests can be done to check for coronavirus antibodies which indicate exposure to a coronavirus. This is not diagnostic of FIP, and it is very common for healthy cats to have positive titres resulting from exposure to feline coronaviruses, which may include FIP. A positive test alone is therefore not a reason for not boarding a cat, or treating it any differently to other cats in the cattery.

Feline leukaemia virus * (FeLV)
Feline leukaemia virus is one of the most important viral infections of cats and is a common cause of illness and death. Persistent infection with the virus results in a number of potential sequelae including severe immunosuppression, anaemia and the development of tumours, all of which are eventually fatal. The virus does not survive well in the environment and is susceptible to common disinfectants, so transfer of infection relies on direct contact between cats, and is therefore not a concern in boarding FeLV-infected cats.

Source and spread of infection
The major source of FeLV is virus shed in the saliva of a persistently infected cat. After prolonged close contact involving mutual grooming or sharing of food dishes, susceptible in-contact cats may be exposed to sufficient virus for them to become infected. Additional exposure to FeLV may also come about through cats biting, as well as contact with faeces and urine in shared litter trays. If an infected queen becomes pregnant, the FeLV infection will probably result in early death of the kittens and their resorption or abortion. Occasionally though, she may give birth to live kittens at full term but these will invariably be infected with the virus. As prolonged contact between cats is necessary for efficient transmission of the virus, infection is more common in situations where there is a high population density of cats and the highest prevalence of infection is often found in multicat households and rescue facilities.

Outcome following exposure to FeLV
Not all cats exposed to FeLV become persistently infected with the virus. Some cats are able to mount an effective immune response that eliminates the virus from the body after a short period of time (transient infection). The age at which a cat is exposed to FeLV has an important effect on the outcome of exposure and this is related to the maturity of the immune system. Young cats, particularly those less than four to six months of age are especially susceptible to the development of persistent infections after exposure to FeLV.

Clinical disease
Persistent FeLV infection usually results in the death of an infected cat. The most common consequence of infection is the development of immunosuppression which can have a profound and devastating effect on an individual cat. This probably accounts for around 50 per cent of the deaths associated with FeLV infection and the clinical signs seen are similar to those with FIV infection. The second most common consequence of FeLV infection is the development of anaemia which is often progressive, resulting in death. Although FeLV is commonly associated with the development of neoplasia (lymphoma and leukaemia), tumours in fact only develop in around 15 per cent of infected cats. Approximately 30 per cent of all feline tumours are lymphomas, and around 70 – 80 per cent of cats that develop lymphoma are found to be infected with FeLV. A further 10 per cent of FeLV-infected cats will develop a variety of problems that are not directly associated with neoplasia, anaemia or immunosuppression; these include fading kittens (when kittens die for no apparent reason), neurological disease, ocular inflammatory disease, severe weight loss and wasting (cachexia) and severe enteritis.

Diagnosis
Diagnosis of FeLV infection is usually straightforward. The most common test is a simple kit which looks for the presence of a viral protein in the blood. A positive test result usually indicates persistent infection but if a healthy cat has a positive test, it is important to repeat the test after a period of time, preferably also sending a blood sample to a reference laboratory where the virus can be isolated from the blood, to confirm that the cat really is persistently infected with the virus. FeLV tests based on examination of saliva rather than blood are not recommended as these are much less reliable.

Control
When FeLV is diagnosed in a cat, the other cats in the

household should be tested for this infection as the consequences of infection are so severe. Sick cats should definitely be tested. If possible and practical, infected cats should be separated from those that are clear of infection. Several FeLV vaccines are now available but none offer complete protection against infection and it is important that a vaccinated cat is not deliberately exposed to FeLV by allowing it to mix with a known infected cat. It is also unwise to assume that a vaccinated cat is necessarily free of FeLV and a vaccination certificate should not be accepted in place of a negative FeLV test.

Cats can be vaccinated against FeLV and several different types of vaccine are now available. The manufacturers of FeLV vaccines recommend that cats and kittens should be tested for FeLV prior to vaccination. This is not because vaccinating a positive cat would be harmful to it but because positive cats derive no benefit from vaccination. Additionally, if a cat is vaccinated but untested, it will not be known if it is safe to introduce it to other cats that are known to be free from infection because it will not be known if the cat is excreting FeLV or not.

Boarding FeLV-infected cats
The major source of FeLV is virus shed in the saliva of a persistently infected cat. FeLV is spread between cats following prolonged close contact such as mutual grooming or sharing of food bowls. A bite from an infected cat or contact with infected urine or faeces in litter trays may also act as routes of exposure to the virus. FeLV-infected cats admitted to a boarding cattery can be housed with other cats from the same household but should not be allowed any contact with other boarding cats. This is a normal requirement for all cats in a boarding cattery, in order to minimise the risk of transmission of all infectious diseases, so should not pose any problems to the cattery owner. Between handling cats from different households, the hands should be washed and there should be no sharing of food bowls or litter trays between different pens.

FeLV-infected cats may appear clinically well in the early stages of disease but, as outlined earlier, severe disease often develops and this may require veterinary treatment and eventually euthanasia. Boarding of FeLV-infected cats may involve administration of medicines and, in general, extra vigilance is required in case illnesses arise when the cat is in the cattery. If in doubt, consult a veterinary surgeon for advice.

Feline panleucopenia *
– see Feline infectious enteritis (FIE)

Feline spongiform encephalopathy (FSE)
This is a rarely diagnosed neurological disease which is very similar to bovine spongiform encephalopathy (BSE). Affected cats may show signs of incoordination, seizures, increased sensitivity to touch or sound, altered behaviour (eg, timidity, aggression) and increased appetite. Unfortunately this is a rapidly progressive and incurable disease. If suspected, a veterinary surgeon should be consulted for advice.

Feline urological syndrome * (FUS)
– see Lower urinary tract disease

Feline viral rhinotracheitis * (FVR)
Another name for feline herpesvirus – see Respiratory disease

Fit
– see Convulsions or Epilepsy

Fleas *
– see Parasites (fleas)

Fracture
Fracture is the medical term for a broken bone. This can be caused by trauma such as a road traffic accident. Pathological fractures are breaks which occur without any trauma and occur in diseased bone. Causes of pathological fractures include cancer and poor nutrition (calcium deficient diet). Cats with fractures usually show signs of severe pain and may not be able to stand or move. Veterinary advice should be sought as a matter of urgency.

Fur balls
A cat which is moulting heavily or grooming excessively will ingest fur that may form a solid ball in the stomach. Fur balls may pass through the bowels normally or be vomited up. In severe cases, they can cause an obstruction and this will need veterinary attention. Proprietary fur ball remedies are available through a veterinary surgeon but quite often a meal of oily fish is all that is required. Regular grooming, particularly of long-haired cats and during moulting periods, will help to avoid the build-up of fur in the stomach.

Giardia
– see Parasites (protozoal organisms)

Gingivitis
– see Mouth problems

Haemorrhage
The medical term for bleeding which can be internal or external. Veterinary advice should be sought immediately.

Hair balls
- see Fur balls

Heart disease *
Cats may occasionally be born with heart conditions (congenital heart disease) such as abnormal heart valves, holes in the heart or abnormal vessels or circulatory pathways. Many of these conditions will be detected when the cat is a kitten although not all of them will significantly compromise the cat which may be able to lead a relatively normal life.

Other heart diseases will develop during the cat's life (acquired heart disease). Most often, these diseases affect the heart muscle causing thickening of this (hypertrophic cardiomyopathy) although a variety of other conditions affecting the heart muscles and valves can be seen. In some cases, the heart disease is secondary to another disease such as hyperthyroidism.

In the early stages of heart disease, affected cats often adjust their lifestyle by spending more time asleep and so it can be difficult to identify cats with heart disease. Clinical signs which often develop later on include lethargy, breathlessness, weight loss and occasional vomiting. High blood pressure and problems with blood clots forming and then blocking blood vessels (thromboembolic disease) can also be seen.

Diagnosis may be suspected on the basis of presence of suitable clinical signs and findings such as a heart murmer, increased or irregular heart rhythm on physical examination. Chest X-rays, electrocardiography (ECG) and ultrasound of the heart are usually needed to make an accurate diagnosis. Measuring blood pressure and examination of the eyes for evidence of high blood pressure is often needed too.

Treatment depends very much on the cause and severity of the heart disease for example, in hyperthyroid cats with heart disease, treatment of the thyroid disease is usually all that is required to reverse the heart disease. In other cats treatment of heart failure using drugs such as diuretics may be needed in addition to drugs which have a specific effect on the heart. Aspirin may also be prescribed at a low dose to help to reduce the risk of thromboembolic disease.

The long term outlook for a cat with heart disease is very variable according to the cause and extent of the heart disease. Some cats may live for many years with significant heart disease while the progression may be more rapid in other cases.

Boarding of cats with heart disease may require administration of medication prescribed by the cat's veterinary surgeon. If signs of congestive heart failure are seen, a veterinary surgeon should be contacted for advice. Congestive heart failure can be treated - most commonly diuretics such as frusemide are used. These signs include:

◆ Lethargy
◆ Breathlessness – particularly urgent if the cat is breathing through its mouth
◆ Cyanosis – blueing of the membranes of the mouth and eyes. An emergency if seen!
◆ Loss of appetite

A veterinary surgeon should also be contacted urgently if:
1 Signs of high blood pressure such as sudden onset blindness are seen. This requires immediate treatment to prevent further damage.
2 Signs of thromboembolic disease are seen. In this situation, a blood clot forms in the abnormally enlarged heart. If the blood clot is released into the circulation, it can block a major artery. The most common location for this to occur is the end of the aorta which is the biggest artery in the body. When the clot blocks the end of the aorta it is commonly referred to as a 'saddle thrombus' because of its appearance. If this happens, the blood supply to the back legs is blocked and affected cats will show signs including:
◆ paralysed hind-limbs which are cold and extremely painful
◆ occasionally one leg may be affected rather than both
◆ a fore-limb may occasionally be affected

Treatment of these cats is often unsuccessful and because the condition is very painful, many owners elect for euthanasia if this is seen. In some cases, nursing and appropriate treatment from a veterinary surgeon (including painkillers) can bring about a complete recovery, although this may take several days or weeks. However, these cats are at a very high risk of having future episodes of thromboembolic disease so the long term outlook is extremely grave.

Hepatitis
– see Liver disease

Hernia
A hernia is a defect in the body wall that results in the abnormal protrusion of tissues. The most commonly occurring hernia is an umbilical hernia which results from a defect in the muscle of the ventral abdomen. Fat and other abdominal contents are able to migrate through this hole and result in a swelling under the skin. Another common site for hernias is the inguinal region (inner thigh area). Hernias are usually easily distinguished from other lumps as they can be reduced

(eg, the lump can be pressed back into the abdomen). Often hernias are congenital (ie, present from birth). They rarely cause clinical problems but should be checked by a vet. If necessary they can often be corrected at the time of routine neutering.

Hyperthyroidism *
Hyperthyroidism is the term used to describe the disease seen in cats producing excessive amounts of thyroid hormones in their thyroid gland. The thyroid is found in the neck, close to the larynx (voice box) and is composed of two lobes – one on each side. Rarely thyroid tissue can be present in other locations ('ectopic') and this too can sometimes become diseased.

Hyperthyroidism is a common condition of middle aged and older cats. Male and female cats are affected with an equal frequency but the disease is less common in some pure breeds such as Siamese. In the vast majority of cases (98 – 99 per cent) the disease is caused by benign overgrowth of thyroid tissue. Rarely (in less than 2 per cent of cases) a malignant cancer is responsible.

The thyroid hormones act on all cells and have many actions, including increasing the metabolic rate. In hyperthyroidism a variety of clinical signs can be seen, most commonly including:-
◆ Weight loss
◆ Voracious appetite
◆ Hyperactivity and irritability
◆ Increased thirst and urination
◆ Gastrointestinal signs such as vomiting or diarrhoea
◆ Coat changes

These signs often worsen with time as hyperthyroidism is a progressive disease. Secondary complications associated with hyperthyroidism may also be seen and include: Cardiac disease – most frequently thickening of the heart muscle, increased heart rate, heart murmer and high blood pressure

Diagnosis
In most cases, diagnosis of hyperthyroidism is straightforward. Affected cats usually have an enlarged thyroid which can be felt when the neck is examined by a veterinary surgeon. Other clinical findings such as weight loss, fast heart rate and the history (eg, voracious appetite reported) may increase the suspicion of this disease, but a blood test is required to confirm the diagnosis. Levels of thyroid hormones in the blood are increased with this disease. Other blood test abnormalities may be found (such as an increase in the liver enzymes) although these are not specific to hyperthyroidism (eg, seen in cats with liver disease).

Treatment
Hyperthyroidism can be treated in three ways:
1 Surgical removal of the abnormal thyroid tissue
2 Medical treatment with anti-thyroid drugs (needed for the rest of the cat's life as they only reduce the production of the thyroid hormones; they do not cure the underlying disease)
3 Treatment with radioactive iodine (available at a limited number of veterinary hospitals). Radioactive iodine selectively destroys abnormal thyroid tissue. Only options 1) and 3) are curative for this disease. The treatment choice is affected by individual cat and owner factors such as whether an anaesthetic (required for surgical treatment) will be safe. In addition to treatment of the thyroid disease, some cats may need additional drugs to manage complicating factors such as high blood pressure and heart disease.

Boarding hyperthyroid cats
In well stabilised cats receiving medical treatment for

hyperthyroidism (usually carbimazole [Neo-Mercazole]; Nicholas) or (methimazole [Felimazole]; Arnolds), it is important to ensure that medication is given as directed by the prescribing veterinary surgeon. This often involves twice or three times daily administration of tablets (see section on medicating cats). Occasional side effects can be seen in cats receiving anti-thyroid drugs such as carbimazole and methimazole. These are usually reversible on stopping treatment and develop within a few weeks/months of starting treatment.

Mild side effects such as poor appetite, vomiting and lethargy are most common and may resolve within a few weeks. More severe side effects seen rarely, include blood cell abnormalities (including reduced levels of white blood cells and platelets), liver problems and skin eruptions. In any cat where side effects to treatment are suspected, or a hyperthyroid cat receiving medication appears unwell, then veterinary advice should be sought.

Sometimes, undiagnosed hyperthyroid cats are admitted to the cattery. They may be showing clinical signs such as those described earlier. If the cat is largely well in itself, it may not be necessary to seek veterinary advice yourself but this should be discussed with the cat's owner on their return.

Iliac thrombosis
This term defines the situation when a blood clot blocks the final portion of the aorta, the major artery of the body. The final portion of the aorta divides into the iliac arteries which supply blood to the hindlimbs and the condition may result in paralysis of the back legs. This condition is seen mainly in cats with heart disease.

Incoordination
Also referred to as ataxia, it includes cats with a swaying or staggering gait, circling or falling to one side, or with a head tilt. These signs may be seen in cats recovering from a convulsion, after an accident or poisoning. They may also be associated with vestibular disease, a disorder of the inner ear affecting balance or can be caused by a variety of severe neurological or circulatory problems. If any of these symptoms develop, seek veterinary advice as soon as possible.

Incontinence
Incontinence may be seen in some cats which have had road traffic accidents. Incontinence pads or sheets can be obtained – these are disposable, absorbent sheets which can be used as a bed or general 'carpet' in the pen. Incontinent cats may need frequent baths to avoid excess soiling of the coat which can cause scalding (urinary incontinence). Faecal incontinence can lead to fly strike (flies laying eggs which hatch into maggots on the cat).

Jaundice
This is the medical term for yellowing of the mucous membranes (gums, third eyelids) and skin. Jaundice is seen in cats that have high blood levels of bilirubin, a red blood cell breakdown product and can occur for three reasons:
◆ Excessive breakdown of red blood cells (haemolysis) eg, due to FIA
◆ Liver disease
◆ Obstruction to the bile duct preventing pigments from entering the bowel
Jaundice is a cause for concern should it develop in a boarded cat and veterinary advice should be sought.

Kidney disease *
Chronic renal failure is one of the most common diseases of older cats and therefore may be present in cats admitted to the cattery. Typically, signs include weight loss, poor appetite, dull coat and increased thirst.

Diagnosis of chronic renal failure (CRF) depends on blood and urine tests which confirm this disease and rule out other causes of weight loss in older cats (such as hyperthyroidism and diabetes mellitus).

Chronic renal failure is an incurable and often progressive disease but appropriate treatment may help to control the clinical signs and improve the well-being of the cat. Various treatments may be indicated; in established cases this often includes feeding a prescription diet which is moderately restricted in protein and phosphorus. Several commercially produced prescription diets are available and cats with CRF admitted to the cattery should continue to be fed on these throughout their stay, as directed by the cat's veterinary surgeon. Some cats find these diets unpalatable so initially, they may need to be mixed with the cat's normal food to encourage acceptance. It is very important that a cat with renal failure has access to fluids at all times and is encouraged to drink. For this reason, tinned foods with their high water content are preferred, but if cats are fed on a dry food, it is important to encourage sufficient fluid intake, and it may help to add some water or gravy to the food. The cat's vet may suggest a variety of other supportive treatments for renal failure depending on the individual case.

Dehydration is a potential complication of CRF and requires urgent treatment. Veterinary advice should be sought in cats with known CRF if they appear dull, depressed, lose their appetite or vomit. Dehydration can be crudely assessed by evaluating skin 'tenting'. A flap of skin, such as that over the scruff, is pinched and lifted up before letting go and watching it return to its normal position. In dehydrated cats, the skin may stay in a 'tented' position or creep slowly back to its normal position, whereas in healthy cats the 'tent' should disappear almost immediately. Dehydrated CRF cats may require intravenous fluid therapy so veterinary advice should be obtained immediately if this possibility is suspected.

Lice
– see Parasites (lice)

Liver disease *
The liver performs vital functions including production of essential blood proteins and clotting factors, removal of waste substances and drugs, and is very important in controlling the normal metabolism of fats, carbohydrates and proteins.

Cats can be affected by congenital (present from birth) and acquired (developing later in life) liver problems. The clinical signs seen in affected cats are variable but include:

◆ altered appetite – decreased with some problems but increased with others
◆ jaundice – yellow discolouration of the skin and membranes of the eyes and mouth (see jaundice)
◆ ascites – fluid build up in the abdomen leading to abdominal distension
◆ increased thirst
◆ gastrointestinal signs such as vomiting and diarrhoea
◆ non-specific signs such as lethargy, weight loss and malaise

Diagnosis
Making a diagnosis often depends on the use of laboratory

tests such as blood tests and liver biopsy. Other tests such as X-rays and ultrasound of the liver may also be helpful.

Treatment
Treatment of liver disease depends on the cause and may include feeding a special diet. Cats admitted to the cattery may need medications and if any deterioration in their condition is seen while they are boarding, it is sensible to consult a veterinary surgeon for advice.

Lower urinary tract disease *
The most common form of urinary tract disease in cats is cystitis or inflammation of the urinary bladder. Typical signs of cystitis include an increased frequency of urination, straining to urinate (sometimes with signs of discomfort) and there may be blood in the urine. Although the presence of

Cat straining to pass urine

blood often looks dramatic, there is rarely any significant blood loss from this route but you should always seek veterinary advice. Cystitis or inflammation of the bladder can be caused by infection, although it is not common for this to be the primary cause. Many cases of cystitis do resolve spontaneously within three to five days. However, if the condition persists or if it recurs within a short period of time, it is essential that the cat is examined by a veterinary surgeon so that any specific underlying cause can be found and treated. Frequent emptying and changing of litter trays is also helpful in encouraging a cat to urinate frequently.

One potential emergency arises when lower urinary tract inflammation leads to blockage of the urethra and an inability to pass urine. This most commonly occurs in male cats and, if a cat repeatedly strains to pass urine but nothing is produced, immediate veterinary attention should be sought because a blocked urethra rapidly progresses to life-threatening acute renal failure or rupture of the bladder. The usefulness of a 'pee and poo' chart becomes very evident in such cases.

Lumps and bumps
Any lumps and bumps should be investigated. If found during the initial examination, they should be discussed with the owner. The owner may be aware of the condition but have forgotten to explain a long-standing problem. If the lump is new, action will have to be taken.

Any lumps which are painful are likely to be inflammatory (eg, abscess) and may need veterinary attention. Small, pain-free lumps are less urgent but advice from a veterinary surgeon should be sought if any rapidly growing lumps are found in case these are cancerous – depending on the

length of the cat's stay. If the cat is only in for a couple of weeks, this can be discussed with the owner on their return.

Lymphoma, lymphosarcoma
This is the most common cancer that cats suffer from. Lymphoma is a malignant cancer of the white blood cells and can be associated with solid lumps in tissue organs (eg, the liver, eyes, kidneys, lymph nodes) or with leukaemia (malignant cells in the bloodstream). Lymphoma can be treated using chemotherapy (oral and injectable anti-cancer drugs) with some cats doing extremely well on this therapy living for many years with no signs of ill health. However, in those cats with leukaemia or very advanced lymphoma, the long term outlook is often very poor.

Megaoesophagus
The oesophagus is the food pipe which propels swallowed food from the mouth to the stomach. In cats with megaoesophagus, the food pipe fails to work leading to the build up of food in the oesophagus. Eventually (usually soon after eating), the food is passively regurgitated. Since the food has not reached the stomach, the cat may try to re-eat this. The regurgitated food is often sausage-like in appearance and may be wrapped in large amounts of thick saliva. Megaoesophagus is a rare condition which some cats, particularly Siamese, may be born with or it can develop later in life. See also oesophageal problems for information on managing cats with this condition.

Miliary dermatitis
This term describes the skin disease which can be seen in cats allergic to fleas. Many small scabs are seen over the body making the skin lumpy when stroked.

Mites
– see Parasites (mites)

Mouth problems *
Weight loss can sometimes be the first sign of oral disease in cats. In some cases, cats may try to eat food but will show signs of oral pain and will possibly salivate excessively. Various problems can arise in the mouth including dental and gum disease, injury such as a lacerated tongue, fractured jaw, cancer, and chronic inflammation.

A build up of tartar and calculus on the surfaces of the teeth

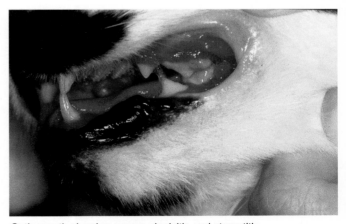

Cat's mouth showing severe gingivitis and stomatitis

is common in cats and, in some cases, may cause or contribute to severe gingivitis (inflammation of the gums) or stomatitis (inflammation of the mouth). The teeth should be inspected and if excessive dental calculus or signs of inflammation are present, veterinary attention should be sought. Calculus tends to accumulate around the junction of the gum with the tooth and, as this occurs, a niche is produced in which bacteria can flourish. In severe cases, as a result of bacterial infection, the gums will become very inflamed and will retract from the base of the tooth. The gums may also become ulcerated and the infection may penetrate further. The retraction of the gum can allow infection to track down the outside of the tooth root (periodontitis) and a discharge of pus (pyorrhoea) from around the teeth may result. The tooth root may also become infected and eroded. Abscesses may also form at the root tip of any tooth and will cause the cat considerable pain and discomfort. Depending on the severity of disease, treatment with antibiotics or other therapies may be necessary. Rarely, severe cases may require an anaesthetic for dental treatment as an emergency, but in most cases this sort of treatment can be deferred until the owner returns and collects the cat from the cattery.

Mycobacterial infection

Cats may become infected with a variety of mycobacterial infections which can affect the skin, lymph nodes and internal organs. Some of these infections are transmissible to people although the risk is generally very low. Skin lesions are most common (and are not usually transmissible to people). These manifest as areas of open sores, scabs or lumps. The closest lymph node may become swollen and affected cats may feel quite depressed and unwell. This type of mycobacterial infection is usually acquired via a bite from a small rodent and can be treated with specific anti-mycobacterial drugs. If a boarding cat develops skin lesions whilst kept, veterinary advice should be sought although if the cat appears otherwise well it may be possible to delay this until the owner returns.

Nasal disease

Cats with diseases of the nose usually show signs including sneezing, snuffles, nasal discharge, difficulty breathing through the nose and may be off their food if their sense of smell is affected.

A variety of causes of nasal disease exist including chronic rhinitis, cancer, foreign bodies (eg, grass) and polyps in the pharynx (area just behind the nose). Polyps are benign growths that may arise following flu virus infection in some cats.

If a cat develops signs of nasal disease whilst boarding, it is prudent to isolate the cat if possible and barrier nurse until veterinary advice has been sought and cat flu can be ruled out as a possibility.

Neoplasia

Persistent, purposeless proliferation of cells. This includes benign and malignant growths. See also cancer and lymphoma.

Obesity *

Very overweight cats may have difficulty jumping or manoeuvring themselves around the cattery unit. Care should be taken to ensure that the cat can easily access its bed, litter tray and food and water.

Obese cats that stop eating are vulnerable to developing a particular sort of liver disease called hepatic lipidosis (fatty liver). This is very severe and can cause death. If an overweight cat stops eating for two or more days whilst boarding, veterinary advice should be sought promptly in order to prevent this from developing.

Oesophageal problems

Occasionally, cats need to be fed from a height if they have oesophageal conditions including megaoesophagus. In this particular condition, the oesophagus (food pipe which carries swallowed food to the stomach) fails to work properly and food accumulates in the oesophagus. Affected cats may regurgitate this food, sometimes with foamy saliva. Regurgitation is a passive process, (unlike vomiting which involves abdominal effort), and since the food has not been digested, the cat may be tempted to re-eat it. Management of this condition includes feeding a diet which the cat is most successful at keeping down (this varies according to each individual) and feeding from a height may also help (gravity helping food to pass down to the stomach). See also – megaoesophagus and vomiting and regurgitation.

Feeding a cat with oesophageal problems from a height may help food to pass down to the stomach

Otitis
– see Ear infections

Otodectes
– see Ear infections and Parasites (mites)

Parasites

The most common parasites to affect cats are fleas, mites, ticks, lice, roundworms and tapeworms. All of these can cause problems, particularly where several cats are kept in a group situation. Fortunately, treatment is usually very simple. Most parasitic infections are contagious and so it is likely that all cats from the same household will be infected and require treatment.

The life-cycle of intestinal parasites can be described as direct or indirect. With a direct life-cycle, eggs are shed in the faeces and then ingested by another cat, providing direct transmission from cat to cat. With an indirect life-cycle, an intermediate host is required. For example, the eggs shed in the faeces may be ingested by a rodent. The parasite may or may not undergo development within the rodent but then another cat becomes infected indirectly, by ingesting the infected rodent.

Parasites: Fleas *

Adult fleas may live for up to a year and have a direct life-cycle, laying eggs either on the cat or in the environment. Larvae hatch from eggs and, as they mature, they form a pupa from which the adult flea eventually emerges. When considering control of a flea problem, it is important to remember that the immature forms of the flea, along with a large number of adults, will be in the environment and not on the cat itself.

Adult fleas are blood sucking insects and can cause physical irritation to the skin resulting in pruritus (itching) and commonly, flea infestation results in the development of a hypersensitivity (allergy) to the flea saliva, causing severe pruritus with excessive grooming, licking and scratching. This may be seen as miliary dermatitis (a papular skin rash along the back of the cat) or sometimes as alopecia (hair loss) due to excessive grooming over the back, flanks and hind limbs. Diagnosis of flea infestation can be made by observation of the fleas, however this can be difficult because cats are such fastidious groomers. If fleas cannot be seen, their droppings (flea dirt) can be found in the bedding or during grooming. If the cat is rubbed over with a damp piece of kitchen towel, flea dirt shows as specks of blood.

As a cattery owner, you should be aware that it is very likely that flea-infested cats will be boarded from time to time. Use of an environmental flea spray, obtained from a veterinary surgeon, is advised to reduce build up of fleas in the cattery environment. This particularly applies to surfaces in the cattery which cannot be washed or thoroughly cleaned. Cracks in wood can potentially harbour fleas and should be treated with an environmental spray, according to the manufacturer's instructions. If fleas are detected on a cat boarding, it is important that veterinary advice is sought on the most appropriate treatment for that cat, bearing in mind if it has been recently treated with any anti-flea preparations. Effective flea treatments are prescription only medicines (POMs) (see section on medicines) and should only be used on the animal for which they were prescribed, following the instructions given by the prescribing veterinary surgeon. For these reasons, it is useful to ascertain when the cat was last treated for fleas, what was used and who prescribed it, when a cat is admitted to the cattery. Because it is a POM the owner's consent should also be acquired before using it – this is the reason for sorting out all such matters on the consent form as the cat is admitted.

Effective flea treatment requires treatment of all cats in the same unit, although care should be taken when treating kittens. A variety of products is available and a suitable regime can be worked out with the help of your veterinary surgeon who has access to products that are far more effective than those purchased from pet shops. Organophosphate insecticides have been widely used in the past but these are potentially toxic and other safer, more effective products are now available such as Frontline (Merial), Advantage (Bayer) and Stronghold (Pfizer). These are 'spot on' preparations which are easy to administer, work quickly and last for a month (see page 90 for administration). 'Stronghold' is used monthly and is effective against fleas, roundworms, hookworms, ear mites, biting lice (eg, *Felicola subrostratus*) and at preventing heartworm. It is safe in lactating and pregnant queens and in kittens from 6 weeks old. Stronghold is not licensed for treatment of ticks, cheyletiella, demodex or sarcoptes. 'Frontline' is effective for ticks and cheyletiella.

The use of flea collars is not advised as these have limited efficacy and ultrasonic flea collars do not work! There is also a danger that collars can get caught on the wire mesh of the run if the cat is an energetic climber. It is usually advisable to remove all collars in the cattery. Follow-up flea treatment, of the cat and the owner's house, may be required once the cat has left the cattery, and should be given as prescribed by a veterinary surgeon.

Parasites: Lice

In contrast to fleas, lice are species-specific parasites that spend their whole life-cycle on the host; they can be passed from one cat to another following direct contact between cats. Severe infestations may cause pruritis (itching). Diagnosis is made by observation of the lice in the hair-coat. All cats in a group should be treated with an appropriate tratement such as Stronghold, obtained through a veterinary surgeon.

Parasites: Mites

Ear mites: Ear mites (*Otodectes cynotis*) are very common and can be diagnosed by a veterinary surgeon using an

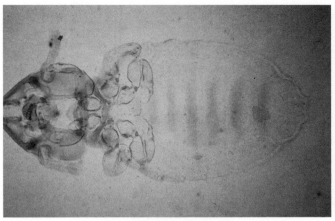

Lice live on cats throughout their whole life cycle and can pass directly between cats

otoscope to examine the ears. In cats infected with ear mites, there is a crusty, granular reddish-brown discharge from the ear which can cause severe irritation. If left untreated, the cat may scratch continuously at the ear and this may result in an aural haematoma developing; this is a large blood blister caused by the rupture of small blood vessels between the skin and cartilage of the ear. Treatment is usually with parasiticidal ear drops – all cats in a group should be treated as mites can move from one cat to another. Occasionally, ear mites will also cause skin disease on the cat and can also affect humans by causing an itchy rash.

Fur mites: This mite is sometimes known as the rabbit fur mite and is called Cheyletiella (pronounced kay – litty – ella). Infestation with this mite often occurs together with dandruff and when severe can look like 'walking' dandruff. It is almost impossible to see the mite without the aid of a good magnifying glass or microscope. It is, however, possible for humans to suffer an irritation through contact with the mites.

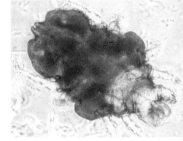

Cheyletiella – sometimes known as rabbit fur mite

*Harvest mites * (Trombicula autumnalis*): These mites appear from July to September and are therefore known as harvest mites. They are not often seen in the northern half of the British Isles. They look like little red spiders and are generally to be found around the cat's ear flap. As the cat scratches, the mites enter the nail bed and settle between the cat's toes. Thus they may spread under its chin, to the base of the spine or on to its chest. This six legged larva feeds on tissue fluid and may cause considerable skin itch and discomfort to cats. The

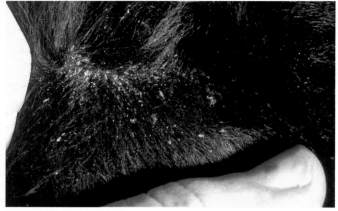
Above: Cheyletiella in the fur of a dog

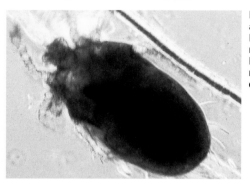

Left: Close up of a harvest mite
Below: Harvest mites on a cat
Bottom: Harvest mite problems on a cat

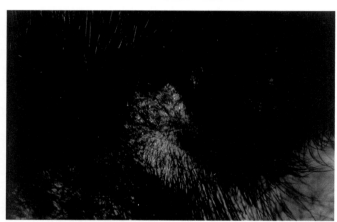

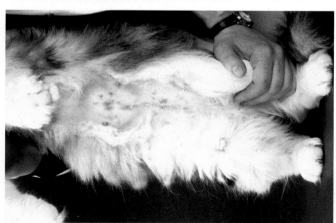

larva feeds by thrusting its small hooked fangs into the surface layers of the skin. It then injects a fluid which breaks down the cells underlying the horny layers of the skin. The liquid food resulting from this process is sucked back into the digestive system of the larva. It will inject and suck for two to three days at the same site until it is replete and has increased in size three to four times. Scratching which may dislodge the mites can result in injury to the skin and in severe cases raw areas can develop These areas can become infected with bacteria.

Treatment options include spraying the cat with flea control products containing fipronil (Frontline; Merial), organophosphates or permethrins. Fipronil spray can be applied every two weeks in this situation to try and deter mites from attaching to the affected parts. A very sensitive cat may have to be confined during the mites' active period and an Elizabethan collar used to prevent further self-inflicted injury to the itchy parts.

Once the cat is in the cattery and has been treated there should be no chance of re-infestation in the run.

Mange mites: Cats may also be infected with various species of mange mites. These cause widespread and severe skin irritation. Veterinary assistance will be required to confirm diagnosis and obtain suitable treatment.

Parasites: Protozoal organisms

A variety of intestinal protozoal (single cell) parasites can also affect cats. The most common of these are known as coccidial parasites. Although infection with coccidial parasites may not be associated with causing illness, kittens in particular may develop diarrhoea, especially if the burden of infection is high. Diagnosis of infection is based on faecal analysis and treatment is usually with sulphonamide-type antibiotics.

Giardia is another protozoal parasite found in the intestinal tract. Diarrhoea is the most common sign and this may be sudden or continue for some time. Faeces are variable but are frequently light in colour, foul-smelling and may be blood-stained. Weight loss and stunted growth may occur in addition to the diarrhoea but loss of appetite is unusual. Giardia is easily transmitted and can be picked up from the environment. It can also be transmitted to humans. Diagnosis requires faecal examination to detect the organism, but treatment with metronidazole or fenbendazole is usually effective.

Parasites: Roundworms *

Roundworms are extremely common internal parasites which inhabit the small intestine from where adults release microscopic eggs into the faeces. Roundworms have a direct life-cycle via eggs shed in the faeces, but indirect transmission can also occur through an intermediate hosts such as a mouse. Nursing queens can also pass on infection to kittens through their milk as they will have parasitic larvae dormant in certain tissues of the body; these larvae migrate to the mammary glands and are then excreted in the milk. This process

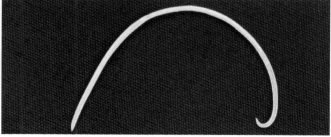

Roundworm – *Picture courtesy of Bayer*

is harmless to the queen but means that kittens are commonly infected from a young age. All kittens will be infected with roundworms. Adult roundworms (producing eggs) may be found in kittens as young as six weeks of age. Severe worm infestation is a potentially dangerous condition in kittens and can cause poor growth, gastrointestinal disturbances and occasionally severe illness which, if left untreated, can lead to death. Diagnosis of infection can be demonstrated when worm eggs or adult worms are seen in a faecal sample and sometimes, where there is heavy infestation, whole worms may be vomited by the cat (these resemble a spoonful of spaghetti!). Often, infected cats show no clinical signs and the presence of the worms can only be detected by microscopic examination of faeces.

If roundworms are suspected, veterinary advice should be sought as to the most appropriate treatment for that cat, bearing in mind if it has been recently treated with any worming preparations. Effective worm treatments are prescription only medicines or pharmacy and merchants list products (see section on medicines) and so need to be obtained from a veterinary surgeon caring for that cat. Worm treatments obtained should only be given to the cat for which they were prescribed, following the instructions given by the prescribing veterinary surgeon. For these reasons, it is useful to ascertain when the cat was last treated for worms, (what was used and who prescribed it), when the cat is admitted to the cattery. Likewise, owner consent for treatment should be acquired. Several worm treatments are available and a veterinary surgeon will be in the best position to advise which is most appropriate for the cat.

Parasites: Tapeworms *

In contrast to roundworms which have shorter (8 to 15 cm) rounded bodies, tapeworms are long (20 to 60 cm) and flat, composed of many individual segments. Mature segments containing eggs are released from the end of the worm into the faeces. These segments are motile (moving) and sometimes look like grains of rice. They can occasionally be seen on the hair around the anus of the cat or in the faeces.

A variety of tapeworms infect cats and all have indirect life-cycles. Cats can become infected with the most common

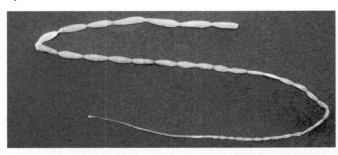

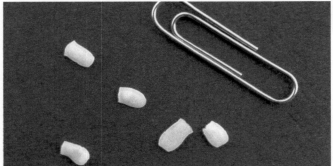

Above: A Whole tape worm. B Tape worm segments – these are often seen in the hair around a cat's tail and look like small grains of rice. *Pictures courtesy of Bayer*

tapeworm *Dipylidium caninum* by ingestion of an infected flea during grooming. Flea infestations are common in cats, tapeworm infestation is also common and it should be assumed that any cat with fleas will also have tapeworm infection. Some cats will also become infected during hunting by eating an infected rodent; infection with tapeworm should be expected in any cat that actively hunts, or has fleas.

If tapeworm infestation is suspected, veterinary advice should be sought as to the most appropriate treatment for that cat, bearing in mind if it has been recently treated with any worming preparations. Effective worm treatments are prescription only medicines or pharmacy and merchants list products (see section on medicines) and so need to be obtained from a veterinary surgeon caring for that cat. For these reasons, it is useful to ascertain when the cat was last treated for worms, (what was used and who prescribed it), when the cat is admitted to the cattery. Owner consent for treatment is also necessary. Several worm treatments are available and a veterinary surgeon will be in the best position to advise which is most appropriate for the cat. Affected cats should also be treated for fleas, under veterinary supervision (see section on fleas).

Parasites: Ticks

Ticks are occasionally found on cats. If just a few ticks are present, these can be removed with forceps or special tick removers. Take great care to remove each one completely. It is very important to ensure that the whole tick is removed, (including the mouth-parts) to avoid causing an infection. This can be very difficult so if in doubt, contact your vet before attempting to remove the tick. If several ticks are present, the cat will need to be treated as for a severe flea infestation using a preparation such as Fipronil spray (Frontline; Merial). Occasionally, a cat will develop nodules at the location of previous tick bites. These nodules are reactions to the tick's bite but are usually self-limiting and do not require special treatment.

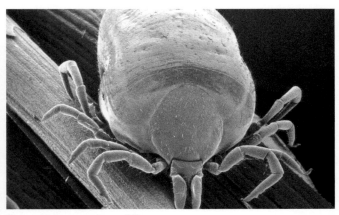

Tick – *Picture courtesy of Bayer*

Parasites: *Toxoplasma gondii* *

Toxoplasma gondii is a common coccidian parasite in cats. It has both a direct and indirect (mainly via rodents) lifecycle and most cats acquire infection when hunting and eating rodents or birds that have the parasite in their tissues. Although infection with this parasite is common, particularly in cats that hunt, clinical disease is very rare. When present, clinical signs include poor appetite, pneumonia, uveitis (inflammation in the eye) and neurological signs. The parasite reproduces in the cat's intestine and forms millions of microscopic eggs (oocysts) which are excreted in the faeces for about two weeks. If the cat uses the garden, as well as a litter tray, the cysts can survive in the soil for many years. Toxoplasma is of major significance because it can be transmitted to humans; children and pregnant women are particularly vulnerable.

Poisoning

Poisoning of cats during their stay at the cattery should not be a problem encountered, but some poisons take a few days to exert their effect and so may be seen in cats after they have been admitted to the cattery. Clinical signs of poisoning include:
◆ Dribbling or foaming at the mouth (hypersalivation)
◆ Vomiting or diarrhoea (especially seen soon after poison ingestion)
◆ Neurological signs such as odd behaviour, seizures
◆ Severe breathing difficulties
◆ Collapse

It is very difficult to confirm poisoning as the cause of illness unless there has been known access to toxic substances or a known drug overdose. If you suspect poisoning, seek urgent veterinary advice.

Poor appetite/reluctance to eat

There may occasionally be a problem with a reluctant eater – for example, a cat being boarded for the first time or a cat which is excessively timid. It may happen with such cats that they will obstinately refuse to eat for a few days, even if offered what has been noted as their favourite food. In such cases, the gentle approach is all important. Serve them small portions of a different food at each meal until one of these triggers a response. This may be a particular tin, some fresh chicken or fish, a favourite biscuit or a few prawns. The addition of a marmite gravy is appetising to some.

Quite often, more timid cats will only eat at night when all else is quiet, so it is important that food should be available to them during this period. However, do be aware that, in the heat of summer, some foods, especially fresh fish, will go off quite quickly. Such dishes must be removed before they cause problems of smell or attract flies. All 'previous day' food dishes, whether empty or not, should be removed in the morning before the breakfasts are served. In some cases, leaving uneaten food with the cat puts the cat off eating completely. Do not let food spoil in warm weather – tinned or wet food will deteriorate much more quickly than dried cat food.

If a cat does not eat for more than two days, a veterinary surgeon should be consulted, as this can itself result in severe illness.

Poxvirus

Feline poxvirus is a member of the orthopoxvirus group and cats are thought to acquire this infection after being bitten by a rodent carrying the virus. Hunting cats are therefore most at risk of acquiring this infection and it is most common in the late summer and autumn when numbers of wild rodents are at their highest.

The first sign of infection is usually a single skin lesion, at the site of the bite, which may appear as a scab or an abscess. This may be itchy causing the cat to scratch or groom this excessively. The most common location for this primary lesion is a forelimb, the head or neck. After a few days to a few weeks, multiple skin lesions develop over the rest of the cat's body. These appear as small lumps which then ulcerate forming a scab which heals to leave a small bald patch. Healing and re-growth of hair is normally complete within two months after the primary lesion was first seen. Because of the delay between

Pox skin lesions on a cat

detection of a primary lesion and development of multiple secondary lesions, it is possible that a cat infected with poxvirus may be admitted to the cattery without the owner's knowledge. Where this infection is suspected, a veterinary surgeon should be contacted for advice.

Infection is not normally too much of a problem to the infected cat unless other diseases such as FeLV or FIV are present, in which case, the infection is more severe and much slower to heal. There are no specific treatments for poxvirus although antibiotic cover may be needed in some cats (especially the FeLV and FIV infected). Treatment with corticosteroids causes severe exacerbation of the infection and can result in the cat's death.

It is possible that people in contact with an infected cat may be affected by this disease. The virus is thought to be spread via cuts or abrasions in the skin and usually a single lesion is noted. Affected people may also suffer from flu-like symptoms such as fever and a headache. Children, the elderly and immunosuppressed people are most at risk and so should avoid contact with a poxvirus infected cat. People caring for cats with poxvirus should wear gloves when handling the cat and follow basic hygiene precautions to avoid spread to themselves or other cats. Although cat to cat transmission has not been proven, this is a possibility. Cats with poxvirus are infectious until the scabs drop off.

Respiratory disease

Respiratory disease is usually divided into lower respiratory tract disease (involving the small airways and lungs) and upper respiratory tract disease, mainly involving the nose and throat.

Lower respiratory tract disease is usually characterised by coughing and, or difficulty with breathing. There is a wide variety of causes including pneumonia and feline allergic airway disease (feline asthma). Cases of lower respiratory tract disease normally require diagnosis and treatment by a veterinary surgeon.

Cat flu or infectious upper respiratory tract disease is a common condition in cats and the vast majority of cases are caused by the cat flu viruses, feline herpesvirus (FHV) and feline calicivirus (FCV). Fortunately, vaccines are available for both of these viruses and this reduces the risk of disease although it is still possible for vaccinated cats to get flu. Only vaccinated cats should be admitted to the cattery, ensuring that vaccination was given at least seven (preferably more) days before admission to the cattery. The major clinical signs of cat flu are sneezing, inflammation of the eyes (conjunctivitis) and nose (rhinitis), with a heavy discharge from the eyes and/or nose that starts off watery and becomes thicker (purulent). Most cats will be dull, depressed, have a poor appetite and a high temperature, and sometimes a cough. Feline calicivirus can cause severe ulceration of the mouth. Occasionally, feline herpesvirus infections can become generalised causing skin lesions and pneumonia. Epidemics of cat flu are uncommon in good boarding catteries, however, vigilance is required to prevent such problems, or to control them as soon as possible should they arise. Kittens, elderly cats, cats with immunosuppressive diseases (such as FeLV or FIV), cats receiving immunosuppressive treatment (such as cats with cancer receiving chemotherapy) and cats with other concurrent diseases are especially susceptible to disease which can be life-threatening.

Cats begin to show signs of cat flu four to ten days after exposure to the virus. During the incubation period, the virus may be spread to many other cats, as during this time the cat appears healthy. Cats incubating the disease may, therefore, appear normal when admitted to the cattery but subsequently become ill and act as a source of infection to other cats in the cattery.

In the long-term, feline herpesvirus and feline calicivirus can cause chronic rhinitis (snuffles), chronic gingivitis (inflammation of the gums) and chronic ocular diseases. Some cats become long-term carriers of the virus. Carriers are cats which appear healthy but are shedding the virus into the environment and acting as a source of infection to other cats. Any cat that has had flu in the past should be treated as a potential carrier of either flu virus so it is important to obtain this information when admitting the cat for boarding. Cats with feline herpesvirus may shed the virus periodically and stress, such as admission to a boarding cattery, is an important trigger factor for reactivation of viral shedding. Cats with feline calicivirus may shed the virus continuously for many months, or longer.

Where an accurate diagnosis is required, swabs are taken from the mouth and sent in virus transport medium to a specialist laboratory.

Treatment
No specific treatments are available for treating viruses but antibiotics to treat secondary bacterial infection can be helpful and veterinary attention should always be sought with cat flu to prevent any serious complications. Good nursing care is very important because dehydration can become a life-threatening problem. Cats often lose their appetite and should be encouraged to eat and drink by offering them slightly warmed, strongly flavoured food, little and often. Finger feeding may be necessary but if a cat fails to eat for two days, veterinary attention should be sought as a matter of urgency. Regular grooming and gentle clearing away of nasal and ocular discharges will also make a cat feel better. Steam inhalation (without decongestants) is also helpful to clear the nasal passages. The cat can be placed in a steamy bathroom or in a pen or wire cat carrier with a bowl of hot water left next to it and both covered with a towel. Doing this for 10 to 15 minutes, two or three times daily is ideal.

Some other causes of respiratory tract diseases need to be seen by a veterinary surgeon; signs to watch out for include discharge or bleeding from a nostril, changes in face shape, particularly swelling and ulceration or erosion of skin around the nose.

As already explained, any cat that has previously had flu should be regarded as a potential carrier of infection to other cats. The stress associated with boarding may precipitate shedding of the virus (in the case of herpesvirus) and thus put other boarded cats at risk of developing flu.

Suspected flu carriers should, as a minimum, be fed and cleaned last to avoid spread of infection. Alternatively, the cat can be placed in the isolation facility and barrier nursed. Flu viruses are able to survive for as long as 10 days on fomites (inert things like food bowls, overalls etc.) so separate food and litter trays should be used for carrier cats and recommendations described in the section on isolation and barrier nursing followed.

Ringworm *
Ringworm is an infection of the skin with one of a group of over 40 fungi (dermatophytes). These fungi invade the superficial layers of the skin, the hair and nails and can

Left: Typical ringworm lesion.

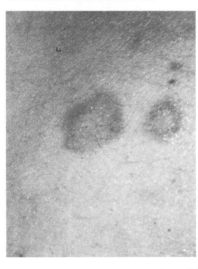
Left: Ringworm on a person - *Picture courtesy of Ann Robinson*

cause disease in both animals and humans. Ringworm is highly contagious in a group of cats and once it is in the environment, can be very difficult to eliminate. It can also be transmitted to humans.

Source and spread of infection
Ringworm is most common in kittens and young cats but can occur in all age groups. Most of the dermatophytes primarily infect the hair shaft and produce a sheath of arthrospores around infected hairs. Vast numbers of these resistant spores are produced and shed into the environment. These spores are the main infectious particle of dermatophytes and cats may become infected, either by direct contact with infected cats, or by sharing the same environment where the arthrospores can survive for 18 months or even longer.

Clinical disease
The incubation period (time from exposure to development of signs) varies from several days to a few weeks. The most common clinical signs are of one or more discrete, irregular

circular areas of alopecia (hair loss) often first seen on the legs or on the head. This hair loss may be accompanied by variable scaling, crusting, thickening and inflammation of the skin. However, a number of other clinical signs may also be seen, including widespread disease (generalised alopecia and scaling), folliculitis (rash), granulomas (lumps) and miliary dermatitis. In some cats, a chronic, localised disease develops with very few, if any observable clinical signs.

If ringworm is suspected on visual examination of a cat prior to admission for boarding, a veterinary surgeon should be consulted as this can be a difficult problem to eradicate once present.

Spontaneous recovery from ringworm usually occurs after three to five months but in some cats, infection may be chronic, lasting many months or years. The variable clinical signs of ringworm are indistinguishable from many other skin diseases and diagnosis relies on the use of specific tests.

Diagnosis
◆ Wood's lamp illumination - a Wood's lamp emits ultraviolet light of a particular wave-length. Infected hairs illuminated with this often produce a yellow-green fluorescence, so examination of the hair-coat, individual lesions, or hairs plucked from lesions under a Wood's lamp can be valuable. However, not all forms of ringworm infection result in fluorescence, so lack of fluorescence does not rule out the diagnosis. The lamp should be allowed to warm up for 5 to 10 minutes prior to use. The examination needs to be performed in a darkened room. True fluorescence of the hairs associated with dermatophytosis must be distinguished from bluish fluorescence produced by the use of topical ointments, or the presence of scales and crusts on the skin. Positive results should be confirmed by microscopy or fungal culture.
◆ Direct microscopy - microscopic examination of hairs or scale is a simple and rapid technique and may be performed at a veterinary surgery or veterinary laboratory. If dermatophyte particles are observed, the diagnosis is confirmed but expertise is required and positive diagnoses are only achieved in around 50 per cent of dermatophyte cases, so once again a negative result does not rule out ringworm infection.
◆ Fungal culture - culture of hairs or scale in the laboratory is the most reliable diagnostic test but may take up to two to three weeks to provide a diagnosis.

Treatment
Treatment is necessary to prevent spread of disease to other animals and humans. Topical treatment (creams and shampoos) can be useful but are usually best combined with a systemic drug given in tablet form. Treatment is usually required for several weeks and when ringworm develops in a group of cats, it is usually necessary to treat the entire group, regardless of whether individual cats have any obvious symptoms.

It is important that environmental contamination with arthrospores is reduced. The hair around individual lesions can be carefully clipped away with scissors and burned. Environmental disinfectants, eg household bleach diluted 1:10 will be helpful to clean the environment, and in addition everything that the cat has come into contact with must be disinfected. These measures should be combined with thorough and regular vacuum cleaning of carpets and furnishings, burning the vacuum bag after use.

Control
Because ringworm is so difficult to treat successfully in a group of cats, it is important to try to prevent its entry. All new cats entering the household should have their hair-coat examined thoroughly and, if any skin lesions are found, veterinary attention should be sought at once to establish if these could be due to ringworm. Because not all strains of ringworm fluoresce, the use of a Wood's lamp should never be used as a substitute for a careful examination of the skin and hair-coat!

Solar dermatitis *
Also known as white ear necrosis, this is a pre-cancerous skin disease seen on the ears, particularly of white cats. Exposure to sunlight is thought to trigger this inflammation which later may progress to squamous cell carcinoma, a skin cancer. The eyelids and nose can also be affected by this disease. Any treatment for solar dermatitis must be provided by the vet. Many owners will use a sun barrier cream; these should be selected with care as not all are suitable for cats. White cats and cats with solar dermatitis should be housed in the shadiest units to keep them as much as possible out of the sun.

Stings
The most common site for stings is on the paws but occasionally, the mouth may be affected. Usually the affected area will swell up very suddenly and the cat may appear subdued. If the head or neck is swollen, seek urgent veterinary advice as breathing may be affected. If a sting is visible, it may be possible to remove this with tweezers. The swelling will usually subside after a few hours but you should consult your vet if the swelling persists or the cat is distressed.

Toxoplasmosis *
– See Parasites (*Toxoplasma gondii*)

Vomiting and regurgitation
Vomiting is a sign of disease and can be caused by a variety of problems that may not necessarily involve the stomach, and may even be unrelated to the intestinal system. It is important to distinguish vomiting from regurgitation of food. Vomiting may be preceded by signs of nausea (eg gulping, miaowing) and involves active abdominal contractions after which the vomit is produced. Vomit may contain bile which is yellow. Regurgitation is the passive process by which food in the oesophagus (food pipe) is brought up. Regurgitated food often looks like the food that was eaten covered with a slimy coating of saliva, and may be tubular in shape. No abdominal contractions are required for regurgitation and since the food has not been digested the cat may try to re-eat this. In general, if a cat vomits occasionally, is not distressed or losing weight and appears normal in all other respects, then there is little cause for concern. If the vomiting starts suddenly but the cat appears otherwise bright, then withdraw food for 24 hours and then feed a light diet such as boiled chicken or fish with rice. Make sure that there is a supply of clean drinking water available. Veterinary advice should be sought urgently if vomiting episodes last for more than 24 hours, there is evidence of intestinal bleeding (seen as either fresh blood in vomit or digested blood which is dark brown and can look like coffee grounds), or if the cat is obviously depressed and unwell. If veterinary assistance is required, it will be helpful to the vet if you know what is being vomited, (eg food, froth or bile) how much and how frequently the cat is vomiting, and the relationship of vomiting to feeding times.

Weight loss
It is not uncommon for some weight loss to be seen in

boarded cats, this may occur because of loss of appetite or stress associated with boarding. In most cases, this is not cause for concern. However, if the cat is staying for longer than a couple of weeks and is continuing to lose weight or if the weight loss is more marked, it may be worth consulting a veterinary surgeon for advice. A veterinary surgeon should also be consulted if the cat refuses to eat for more than two days as this can itself cause severe illness.

Weight loss can accompany a huge variety of different diseases and sometimes it may be the only obvious sign that there is something wrong. Distinction must be made between a cat that refuses to eat and one that is unable to eat because of illness, bad teeth or mouth problems such as ulcers. Loss of appetite is often the first sign that a cat is unwell.

In any cat with signs of weight loss, it is important to determine whether food intake is normal. The cat should be observed eating to see if it has any difficulty or pain and to ascertain how much is eaten. The frequency and consistency of the faeces should be noted and also whether there is any vomiting. All this information will be helpful to your vet in trying to diagnose the underlying cause of the weight loss.

Typical causes of severe weight loss include hyperthyroidism (overactive thyroid), chronic renal failure, gastrointestinal diseases, cancer, diabetes mellitus, and viral infections such as feline leukaemia, feline immunodeficiency and feline infectious peritonitis; all require veterinary diagnosis and treatment.

CHAPTER 20

Health of boarded cats
A little more care - behaviour problems and special cats

The majority of cats boarded present little or no problem to the boarding cattery proprietor in terms of behaviour problems or special requirements. Bearing in mind that the cat has been wrenched from its home, driven miles in a basket and deposited in a totally strange environment among people it does not know, it is perhaps surprising how soon and how well most of them settle. Indeed, cats are known to be more attached to their territory than their owners, so the wrench must be quite large and cats, like people, vary in their ability to cope with change. Some will feel stress more than others and likewise some will react to the stress in a different way to others. Thus if you can get a cat to settle in your cattery and it is happy to be there, it will probably settle much more quickly and easily on a second and third visit. Owners who find that their cats settle well will want to use the cattery again and again. Thus, how you approach cats and help them if required, is important to their wellbeing and to your business. As mentioned above, most cats settle well. Chapter 14 looks at how cats should be handled and approached in general. This chapter looks at some of the more difficult cases and situations where the care of the cats may need a more thoughtful approach.

Boarding cats that have lived abroad
Some infectious diseases not present in this country are found in countries outside the UK and cats which have previously travelled to these may be at risk of them. With the new Pet Travel Scheme (PETS) cats can go on holiday with their owners or can be brought in from certain countries without going through quarantine. Depending on the country, the type and risk of these varies but it is essential that the boarding cattery owner is aware of this possibility when they admit the cat. If the cat subsequently develops any signs of illness, a veterinary surgeon should be contacted and they should be given the following information:

◆ where the cat lived when it was abroad
◆ how long it was in each of these places
◆ when was the cat living in each of these places
◆ any knowledge of 'exotic' infections (ones not present in the UK) in this cat or other animals belonging to the owner

Spread of infection between cats in the cattery is not thought to be a problem provided that normal routine hygiene precautions are maintained.

Elderly cats
Like people, cats experience old age in their own individual ways. The elderly cat requires special provision. As cats age, their body functions change and all of their body systems are affected. Early detection and treatment of disease are important. Since their resistance is often reduced, older cats may be susceptible to disease. Even though medication is available for a wide variety of diseases and conditions, each case must be viewed individually so that quality of life can be maintained for as long as possible. Elderly cats are sometimes intolerant of handling or environmental change; they sleep more, are less active and may appear irritable. The elderly cat may suffer from arthritis resulting in lameness, stiffness, or reluctance to move as well as a variety of other chronic conditions. Elderly cats require easy access to a warm, draft-free bed, which must be placed where they can comfortably sleep without disturbance. Ready access to a cat litter tray is essential. Environmental stress must be kept to a minimum.

Elderly cats will probably not groom themselves well and regular grooming helps to prevent the build up of hairball in the stomach and intestine as well as benefiting the cat's sense of well-being.

Common health problems in older cats include:
◆ Dental disease resulting in gingivitis/stomatitis
◆ Chronic renal failure)
◆ Hyperthyroidism
◆ Constipation

Elderly cats may be admitted with ongoing medical problems requiring feeding of special diets or administration of tablets, etc, (see Chapter 18), as directed by the prescribing veterinary surgeon. Development of new problems in previously healthy elderly cats requires more urgent veterinary attention, so if concerned, discuss things with your vet.

Because they are less active, some older cats may become overweight. Engaging the older cat in moderate play sessions will give him some exercise and an interest that will help bring back a bit of the kitten into his life – not even a senior citizen can resist playing with a piece of string!

Entire cats
Boarding entire cats can cause problems. Entire toms are likely to spray in their pens and the smell would not be

helpful in the proprietor's aims of presenting a clean and hygienic cattery! Boarding entire toms is not recommended.

Entire queens too can cause problems if they are old enough to start calling. They may also spray in the desire to find a mate and both the sounds and smells can cause upset in the cattery.

Pregnant cats
There should be no problem in boarding pregnant cats so long as they are not close to kittening time. Few boarding cattery proprietors would want to have the responsibility of a cat giving birth in the cattery and the care requirements which may go with this if problems arise. However, proprietors may want to have some sort of agreement with the owner to cover any problems – forseen or unforseen regarding the pregnancy.

Kittens
Very young kittens (over 6 weeks) could be boarded if absolutely necessary but they would need to be boarded with their mother and to be kept in isolation for their own safety from infection as they will not have been vaccinated and the protection they receive from their mother's colostrum may be waning. Again, the proprietor would need to sit down with the owner and talk through all the potential problems, how they would be handled and who would pay!

It is possible to board young kittens which have gone to their new homes but remember that they must be fed more frequently, receiving at least four meals a day. Special kitten diets are available. Plenty of toys will help keep a kitten amused while confined in a boarding cattery. However, young kittens can get themselves into all sorts of trouble – curiosity, a small flexible body and lots of energy can be a dangerous combination! Make doubly sure the cat unit is safe and secure and that the equipment/electrical supply etc is safe. Kittens will have to be around 13 to 14 weeks old to have had their complete set of vaccinations with a week or so for them to develop their immunity fully.

Long term boarders
Give extra attention to long term boarders. They can go through a period when they seem depressed. Unless it seems bad enough for a vet or is accompanied but loss of appetite etc, it is likely to be boredom. They may well be missing a run around their garden. Position a long term boarder as near as possible to the area of your cattery where there is most activity - the coming and going will keep it interested and will give all those in the cattery a chance to speak to the cat often.

Recognition of stress
Cats are usually bonded to their environment and so removing them from home will be the cause of some stress. However, cats are also very adaptable and, as most cattery proprietors will tell you, most will settle very well, especially on subsequent visits. Put any one of us in an environment we are not familiar with and we will feel stressed. Some of us will eat more, some will not feel hungry at all for a while – some will become active, some sit very quietly in the corner, some will be noisy, some withdrawn – cats are the same. As we know, cats vary in their characters considerably. Each cat will react differently. Proprietors can do some things to reduce the stress and help the cats to relax. As you become more experienced at cat watching you will be able to pick up the signs of stress – these can range from not eating to aggression or complete withdrawl and all stages in between. Some stressed cats will remain at the back of their pen and show defensive behaviour. They may try to huddle down and make themselves a small as possible. They will probably sit with their ears flattened and their pupils dilated. They may hiss or growl if approached and try to retreat even further.

You will also be able to pick up the signs of recovery as the cat becomes more relaxed. It takes a little time and lots of 'cat watching' and a 'feel' for the cats.

◆ For very nervous or distressed cats ask the owner to ensure they bring bedding and toys from home. Proving something which smells of home and so is familiar in the face of all the new sights, sounds and smells will help considerably.

◆ Make sure the cat has the food it is used to – again familiarity will bring some comfort. If given the choice, a stressed cat will usually choose food which it recognises over something new.

◆ Make sure the cat has somewhere to hide so that it can come to terms with its new environment slowly – it may want a covered bed or litter tray or a box to hide in for a while.

◆ Keep to the routines in the cattery. Once the cat knows what to expect, it will be much less fearful – they very quickly cotton on to feeding times etc and knowing what is going to happen next will help considerably.

◆ Do not force handling – cats do not appreciate being chased or forced to accept attention. Given the option they may try and remove themselves from the situation. Make short quiet visits and use food as a reward for interaction.

◆ Try using one of the feline pheromones which it is suggested has a relaxing affect on the cats – Feliway is available from veterinary surgeons and may help with very stressed cats.It can be sprayed in the cat unit.

Nervous cats
Nervous cats may suffer from stress both because they have been subjected to a journey but also because they have been transported into the alien environment of the cattery. It is important to help them to settle as quickly as possible.

For the first couple of hours leave the cat quietly alone. This does not mean ignore the cat! A small amount of its favourite food may persuade a reluctant eater to begin eating, the first step towards settling in. Large meals may well be off-putting. Thereafter, be particularly quiet, gentle and slow-moving in its presence until it begins to find the courage to behave normally. Give the cat a chance to settle. Given the right approach many such cats will come around and realised that they unit is a very safe place to be and they are warm and comfortable – life here isn't so bad after all.

Aggressive cats
There are a few cats which deal with their fears by being aggressive – luckily these are in a very small minority. Some will only be aggressive if approached or handled. Others may be more proactive and proprietors need to take a great deal of care. If younger or less experienced staff usually deal with the cleaning it may be sensible to tell them that you will deal with this particular cat for the safety of all concerned. A warning should be placed on the run door on the daily record sheet so that everyone is aware of the danger. A cat can cause a great deal of damage, so always approach such cats with extreme care. Move slowly and quietly. Keep

your face turned away when anywhere near the cat, particularly if it is sitting on a shelf. Occasionally, if the cat remains in its chalet during cleaning, the dust pan may be used as a shield to protect the hands while washing the floor in the vicinity of the cat. If the cat is in the run, the presence of a second person, outside the wire, to talk to and distract it can be helpful.

In some cases it may be necessary to adapt the cleaning routine because the disruption of turning everything out every day may cause a stressed cat to become more stressed.

If the cat is obviously disturbed or aggravated by being able to see the other cats you may wish to put something to bar the view and hopefully calm the cat somewhat.

If the cat does bite anyone then they should wash the wound immediately and go to their GP. Cat bites very often become infected and antibiotics are required (see page 77.

Soiling or spraying problems

Few owners will tell you if their cats have spraying or soiling problems in the house at home for fear of being turned away. However, you fill find that, even if you know which ones they were, they are unlikely to do this in the cattery. Often such problems are associated with insecurity in the home – other cats coming in or problems with cats outside, changes to the house, building works etc. One of the ways behaviourists tackle such problems is to use an indoor crate or kittening pen so that the cat is confined in a safe and secure area with its litter tray and bed. Here it can relearn to use the litter or will not feel the need to spray because its environment is safe and predictable. Enlarge a kittening pen a little and you will get a boarding cattery unit! Cats usually behave very well in the unit, not feeling the need to mark their territory or to toilet behind the settee because they are feeling insecure.

Warring cats

Occasionally two cats, or cats within a family group, will not get on. While the odd hiss at each other may be tolerable, any fighting or likelihood of injury must be dealt with quickly. If cats do come in together it is worth discussing how well they get on together. You should have some wording in your agreement which allows you to separate the cats if necessary for their own safety - this should also be discussed with their owner, just so you are covered.

Relevant legislation

Animal Boarding Establishments Act 1963: The Act relates to the running of kennels and catteries.

Chartered Institute of Environmental Health (CIEH) Model Licence Conditions and Guidance for Cat Boarding Establishments (1995): Guidance for local authorities. www.cieh.org

Consumer Protection Act 1987: The Act relates to liability for defective products, consumer safety and misleading price indications.

Control of Substances Hazardous to Health (COSHH) Regulations 1999: COSHH requires employers to weight up the risks to the health of their employees arising from exposure to hazardous substances and to prevent, or where this is not reasonably practicable, adequately control exposure.

Controlled Waste Regulations 1992: These regulations relate to the safe disposal of animal and clinical waste.

Data Protection Act 1998: The Act regulates records of personal data on living individuals kept by electronic methods on personal computers, word processors and mainframe computers. Information from the Office of the Information Commissioner. www.dataprotection.gov.uk

Disability Discrimination Act 1995: The Act relates to discrimination against disabled people.

Electricity at Work Regulations 1989: The Act relates to the safety of electrical fittings and equipment.

Environmental Protection Act 1990: Relates to disposal of waste. (See also Controlled Waste Regulations 1992)

Health and Safety at Work Act 1974: The Act relates to the general duties which employers have towards employees and members of the public, and employees have to themselves and to each other.

Supply of Goods and Services Act 1982: Sets the seal to control all aspects of the relationships between consumers and those who supply them with goods and services. It relates to the transfer of property in goods (there are exceptions), contracts for the hire of goods, and the supply of services.

Trade Descriptions Act 1968 and 1972: The Trade Descriptions Act 1968 as amended is a general Act applying to all who trade in goods (and offer services).

Unfair Contract Terms Act 1977: The Act seeks to mitigate the worst effects of objectionable exclusion clauses by restricting the extent to which liability can be avoided for breach of contract and negligence.

This is not a definitive list

Useful website addresses:

www.hmso.gov.uk
Information on UK Acts of Parliament.

www.hse.gov.uk/pubns
Information on all aspects of Health and Safety in the work place.

www.defra.gov.uk/animalh/
Information relating to quarantine, pet passport scheme, foot & mouth, etc.

Fibreglass cat units with wood or galvanised runs
"Pet Homes"
Mount Pleasant
Hunmanby Road
Reighton
North Yorkshire YO14 9RT
Tel: 01723 892332
Website: www.pethomes.me.uk

Useful addresses

CATTERY BUILDERS (& BUILDING MATERIALS)

PVCu catteries
Pedigree Pens Ltd
Unit A2 Northway Trading Estate, Northway Lane,
Tewkesbury, Gloucestershire GL20 8JH
Tel & Fax: 01684 299567
Website: www.pedigreepens.co.uk

Tudor Fabrications
Sealey's Lane, Parson Drove, Wisbech,
Cambridgeshire PE13 4LD
Tel & Fax: 01945 701186
Website: www.tudor-fabrications.co.uk

Timber Catteries
Classic Catteries
4 Engine Lane, Nailsea,
North Somerset BS48 4RM
Tel & Fax: 01275 810338
Email: chriscadwgan_classiccatteries@hotmail.co.uk

Lindee Lu Limited
Unit 5, Coates Industrial Estate, Southfield Road,
Nailsea, Bristol BS48 1JN
Tel: 01275 853800
Fax: 01275 858496
Website: www.lindee-lu.co.uk

A Neaverson & Sons Ltd
Peakirk, Nr Peterborough,
Cambridgeshire PE6 7NN
Tel: 01733 252225
Fax: 01733 252121

Welland Timber Products Ltd
Iron Pit Close, Geddington Road, Corby,
Northamptonshire NN18 8ET
Tel: 01536 201992
Fax: 01536 401178
Website: www.wellandtimber.co.uk

BUILDING MATERIALS/PRODUCTS

Galvanised wire mesh panels manufactured to customer's specifications (suitable for outdoor runs and safety corridors)
Arkinstall Limited
6 Buntsford Park Road, Bromsgrove,
Worcestershire B60 3DX
Tel: 01527 872962
Fax: 01527 837127
Website: www.arkinstall.co.uk

Durable plastic board/sheeting for lining purposes
Centriforce Products Ltd
14-16 Derby Road, Liverpool L20 8EE
Tel: 0151 207 8109
Fax: 0151 298 1319
Website: www.centriforce.co.uk

Welded mesh, pvc roofing, building products
Moncasters Wire Products (MWP) Ltd
Tattershall Way, Fairfield Industrial Estate,
Louth, Lincolnshire LN11 0YZ
Tel: 01507 600666
Fax: 01507 600499
Website: www.moncaster.co.uk

Polycarbonate sheeting/roofing
Rockwell Sheet Sales Ltd
Rockwell House, Birmingham Road, Millisons Wood,
Coventry CV5 9AZ
Tel: 01676 523386
Fax: 01676 523630
Website: www.rockwellsheet.co.uk

Floor and wall finishes (Specialist)
Compotect
Compotect House, 6 Kelvin Road, Elland HX5 0LL
Tel: 01422 376804
Fax: 01422 257094

Flowcrete UK Ltd
Booth Lane, Sandbach
Cheshire CW11 3QF
Tel: 01270 753000
Fax: 01270 753333
Website: www.flowcrete.co.uk

Epoxy Resin Floor Systems
Tel: 0121 505 3411
Website: www.epoxyresinfloorsystems.co.uk

Renotex Ltd
Pollard Street, Lofthouse Gate,
Wakefield,
West Yorks,
WF3 3HG
Tel: 01924 820003
Fax: 01924 829529
Website: www.renotex.co.uk

Robex Industrial Products Ltd
Knowl Piece, Wilbury Way
Hitchin SG4 0TY
Tel: 01462 422260
Fax: 01462 422262

PAINT MANUFACTURERS

Cuprinol
Cuprinol Ltd (ICI Paints)
Wexham Road, Slough, Berks SL2 5DS
Tel: 01753 550555
Website: www.cuprinol.co.uk

Sadolin
AKZO Nobel Specialist Coatings Woodcare Advice Centre
Meadow Lane, St Ives, Cambs PE27 4UY
Tel: 01480 484262
Fax: 01480 496801
Website: www.sadolin.co.uk

Blackfriar Paints
Tor Coatings Ltd
Portobello Industrial Estate, Birtley
Chester-Le-Street, Co. Durham
DH3 2RE
Tel: 0191 411 3146
Fax 0191 411 3147
Website: www.blackfriar.co.uk

DISINFECTANTS

GPC8
Evans Vanodine International Plc
(Contact for local distributor)
Brierley Road, Walton Summit,
Preston, Lancashire PR5 8AH
Tel: 01772 322200
Fax: 01772 626000
Website: www.evansvanodine.co.uk

Safe4 Solutions
Bostock Road
Winsford CW7 3BD
Tel: 0845 006 2020
Website: www.safe4disinfectant.co.uk

Trigene Advance
Medichem International (Marketing) Ltd
(Contact for local distributor)
PO Box 237, Sevenoaks, Kent TN15 0ZJ
Tel: 01732 763555
Fax: 01732 763530
Website: www.medichem.co.uk

Virkon S & Other Products
Antec International Ltd
Chilton Industrial Estate, Sudbury CO10 2XD
Tel: 01787 377305
Fax: 01787 310846
Website: www.antecint.co.uk

CAT CARRIERS, FOLD-DOWN CAGES

Shaws Pet Products Ltd
Bob Martin (UK) Ltd
Wemberham Lane, Yatton, Bristol BS49 4BS
Tel: 01934 831000
Fax: 01934 831055
Website: www.shawspet.co.uk

MDC Exports Ltd
Unit 11, Titan Court, Laporte Way,
Luton LU4 8EF
Tel: 01582 655600
Fax: 01582 613013
Website: www.mdcexports.co.uk

CAT FLAPS

Staywell, Reilor Ltd
Astra Business Centre, Roman Way,
Preston, Lancs PR2 5AP
Tel: 01772 793793
Fax: 01772 797877
Website: www.reilor.co.uk

CAT LITTER

'Mikki' Litter & Tray (for diabetes samples)
MDC Exports Ltd
Unit 11, Titan Court, Laporte Way,
Luton LU4 8EF
Tel: 01582 655600
Fax: 01582 613013
Website: www.mdcexports.co.uk

Smart Cat (wood pellets)
Spatrek Ltd
Tunstall Road, Bosley,
Nr Macclesfield SK11 0PE
Tel: 01260 223284
Fax: 01260 223589
Website: www.spatrek.co.uk

Snowflake (wood pellets)
Snowflake Pet Products Ltd
Marsh Lane, Riverside Industrial Estate, Boston PE21 7ST
Tel: 01205 311332
Fax: 01205 357974
Website: www.snowflakepets.co.uk

Other brands:
Thomas cat litter/Catsan/Sophisticat
Products available through petshops/supermarkets/
discount stores

COMPUTER CATTERY SOFTWARE

PetAdmin
Woodhouse Technology Ltd
Woodhouse, Woodhouse Lane, Little Waltham,
Chelmsford, Essex CM3 3PW
Tel: 01245 362211
Website: www.petadmin.com

'Petsaway'
Cybertrak Software Ltd, Unit 10, Arundel Mews, Arundel
Place, Brighton, East Sussex BN2 1GG
Tel: 01273 224909
Website: www.cybertraksoftware.com

'Cat-a-log'
Datahub, 69 High Meadows, Compton,
Wolverhampton, WV6 8PP
Tel: 01902 570130
Website: www.datahub.co.uk

DISPOSABLE FEEDING DISHES

(i.e Foodtainer 60)
Omni-Pac UK Ltd
Marine Parade, South Denes, Gt Yarmouth NR30 3QH
Tel: 01493 855381
Fax: 01493 858464
Website: www.omni-pac.biz

Also distributed by:
Southern England:
Dispak Ltd
Lysander Road, Bowerhill Estate, Melksham SN12 6SP
Tel: 01225 705252
Fax: 01225 706915
Website: www.dispak.co.uk

Midlands & North:
Dispak (Midlands) Ltd
Prees Industrial Estate, Shrewsbury Road,
Whitchurch SY13 2DJ
Tel: 01948 841188
Fax: 01948 841187
Website: www.dispak.co.uk

GREENHOUSE SHADING

(Strong sunlight protection)
Products available through garden centers/ DIY stores

INCINERATORS

Incinco
Unit 1, 113-115 Codicote Road, Welwyn AL6 9TY
Tel: 01438 821000
Fax: 01438 820888
Website: www.incinco.com

INDUSTRIAL WIPES ETC

Mullett & Co UK Ltd
Building 3, Gypsy Lane, Frome, Somerset BA11 2NA
Tel: 01373 455665
Fax: 01373 455667
Website: www.mullettand.co.uk

PLASTIC BEDS, TOYS ETC

Catac Products Ltd
3-5 Chiltern Trading Estate, Earl Howe Road
Holmer Green, High Wycombe, Bucks HP15 6QT
Tel: 08453 707040
Fax: 08706 207041
Website: www.catac.co.uk

THERMOSTATS (DIGITAL)

Timeguard Ltd
Victory Park, 400 Edgeware Road, London NW2 6ND
Tel: 020 8450 8944
Fax: 020 8452 5143
Website: www.timeguard.com

VETBED BEDDING

Petlife International Ltd
Minster House, Western Way, Bury St Edmunds IP33 3SP
Tel: 01284 761131
Fax: 01284 761139
Website: www.petlifeonline.co.uk

HEATING EQUPMENT

Infrared heaters (dull emitters)
Diamond Edge Ltd
126 Gloucester Road, Brighton, BN1 4BU
Tel: 01273 605922 + 683988
Fax: 01273 625074
Website: www.diamondedgeltd.com

Servitherm panel heaters
Morgan Hope Industries Ltd
Units 5 & 6, Blowick Industrial Park, Crowland Street,
Southport, Merseyside PR9 7RU
Tel: 01704 512000
Fax: 01704 542632
Website: www.morganhope.com

Flexel ceiling/wall cassettes
Flexel International Ltd
Queensway Industrial Estate, Glenrothes, Fife KY7 5QF
Tel: 01592 757313
Fax: 01592 754535
Website: www.flexel.co.uk

Tubular Heaters
Tubeheat Ltd
Unit 15, Tile Cross Trading Estate, Tile Cross Road,
Birmingham B33 0NW
Tel: 0121 779 5253
Fax: 0121 779 2867
Website: www.tubeheat.co.uk

KENNEL & CATTERY INSURANCE

Brooks Braithwaite (Sussex) Ltd
Unit 4, Bridge Road Business Park, Bridge Road,
Haywards Heath RH16 1TX
Freephone: 0800 626012
Tel: 01444 412118
Fax: 01444 416 878
Website: www.brooksbraithwaite.com

Cliverton
Tittleshall, Kings Lynn, Norfolk, PE32 2RQ
Tel: 01328 702010
Fax: 01328 700155
Website: www.cliverton.co.uk

NFU Mutual
National Company - check website for local contact details
Freephone: 0800 3164661
Website: www.nfumutual.co.uk

Pet Plan Group Ltd
Computer House, Great West Road, Brentford TW8 9DX
Tel: 0845 077 1934
Website: www.petplan.co.uk

WHOLESALERS/CASH AND CARRY

Batleys Head Office (National)
977 Leeds Road, Deighton, Huddersfield HD2 1UP
Tel: 01484 481 150
Website: www.batleys.co.uk

Bookers Head Office (National)
Equity House, Irthlingborough Road, Wellingborough,
Northants NN8 1LT
Tel: 01933 371000
Fax: 01933 371010
Website: www.booker.co.uk

PUBLICATIONS

Kennel & Cattery Management
Albatross Publications, PO Box 523,
Horsham, West Sussex
RH12 4WL
Tel: 01293 871201
Fax: 01293 871301
Website: www.kenelandcattery.com

Your Cat
Roebuck House,
33 Broad Street, Stamford,
Lincolnshire PE9 1RB
Tel: 01780 766199
Fax: 01780 766416
Website: www.yourcat.co.uk

Cat World
Ancient Lights,
19 River Road, Arundel,
West Sussex BN18 9EY
Tel: 01903 884988
Fax: 01903 885514
Website: www.catworld.co.uk

WASTE DISPOSAL SERVICES

Biffa Waste Services Ltd
Head Office, Coronation Road, Cressex,
High Wycombe HP12 3TZ
Tel: 01494 521221
Fax: 01494 463368
Website: www.biffa.co.uk